Graham Gunn is a management and feng shui consultant. He is based in London, England with Integral Dynamics U.K., – a research-based organisation that integrates a wide range of modern sciences and ancient wisdom, related to enhancing personal health and performance.

Although he has been a student of Oriental philosophies for thirty years, his professional background is in the management of high-technology, multinational projects in Europe and the USA. He became interested in linking feng shui with modern research into living and working environments when faced with the problems of reducing the psychological stresses on astronauts for Europe's first manned spacecraft. Thereafter he applied these ideas to high-stress project office environments, schools, land development sites, homes and a host of small and large businesses.

Graham Gunn is a frequent contributor to the media on feng shui matters and is also the author of *Office Feng Shui – in a week*. He is a founder member and former chairman of the Feng Shui Society and holds workshops and courses on practical feng shui and its applications in the UK and other parts of Europe.

Also available in Orion paperback

APPLES & PEARS
Gloria Thomas

ARE YOU GETTING ENOUGH?
Angela Dowden

AROUSING AROMAS
Kay Cooper

COPING WITH YOUR PREMATURE BABY
Penny Stanway

EAT SAFELY
Janet Wright

THE GOOD MOOD GUIDE
Ros & Jeremy Holmes

HEALTH SPA AT HOME
Josephine Fairley

JUICE UP YOUR ENERGY LEVELS
Lesley Waters

SENSITIVE SKIN
Josephine Fairley

SPRING CLEAN YOUR SYSTEM
Jane Garton

HARMONISE YOUR HOME

GRAHAM GUNN

An Orion Paperback
First published in Great Britain in 1999 by
Orion Books Ltd,
Orion House, 5 Upper St Martin's Lane,
London WC2H 9EA

A CIP catalogue record for this book is available from the British Library.

ISBN: 0 75281 665 9

Printed and bound in Great Britain by
The Guernsey Press Co. Ltd, Guernsey, C.I.

CONTENTS

PREFACE

The environments in which we live and work play a significant part in our personal vitality and our sense of harmony with the rest of the world. In my work as a business and project management consultant and as a feng shui consultant, I frequently get involved with people in very complex situations which certainly need additional outside support to get them resolved. However, much of my time, and their money, is spent on discussing quite basic issues around creating an environment that supports their needs, or which at least does not sabotage them. When we have reached some degree of environmental stability or equilibrium it becomes practical and efficient to deal with more complex issues directly, and to make those key adjustments that turn a flat or negative situation into one that is dynamic and positive.

The good news is that a great deal of harmonising can be done at very little or no cost – all you need is the will power to go for more health, comfort and efficiency. The purpose of this book therefore is to spread the word on how you can create for yourself a basically harmonious home environment. The way is then clear for building the general quality or experiences of life that you want, and if you still need outside help, you will get a much better and faster return on your investment.

Make those key adjustments that turn a flat or negative situation into one that is dynamic and positive

CHAPTER ONE

A sense of harmony

Hello, how are you? I mean how do you really feel at this moment. Are you comfortable, worried, irritated, happy, content, bored, sleepy, excited, energetic?

Now look around you and try to evaluate how much the environment you are in is contributing to the feelings that you have. For example you may be in a place that is noisy, untidy and full of traffic fumes, or somewhere that is clean, elegant, quiet and sweet smelling. You may be surrounded by soft colours and peaceful scenes or by harsh colours and aggressive images. How does your particular environment influence your feelings?

Now consider the important issues or challenges you are dealing with in your life at this moment in time. They may be concerned with your close relationships, your wider family, financial problems, job prospects, health, college exams, etc. Can you see that the situations we face today are mostly the direct result of decisions we made in the past? While we may believe that our decisions were based purely on facts and good intentions, it is very probable that they were strongly influenced by how we felt at the time. But we have already seen that how we feel is affected by the environment around us. Just look around you at the people who seem to lurch from crisis to crisis; never able to escape the spiral of disasters. Now look at the environment in which they are making their decisions – it probably looks chaotic too.

So, if we want to change the quality of our life, we need to change the quality of our decisions, so that they are in harmony with what we really need rather than what our surface feelings and emotions dictate. And to help us do that we need to create the right kind of physical environment, and our most important environment is called 'home'.

The Oxford dictionary definition of harmony is 'a state of being which is a consistent or orderly or pleasing or agreeable whole; concordant; free from dissent or ill-feeling'. But what does harmony mean in relation to homes? In my view, a harmonious home means that its physical characteristics support you in getting in touch with your true Self and in making sound decisions that are not distorted by stress and exhaustion.

To change the quality of our life, we need to change the quality of our decisions

Three primary steps will help you to achieve this desirable state:

1 Eliminate or reduce any features that induce negative stress or drain energy.
2 Make specific physical changes to create features that harmonise with your true needs and desires.
3 Keep track of the changes occurring in your life, and adjust your environment accordingly.

Disharmonious aspects of our home can create negative stresses and energy-draining conditions. These can cause, or at least contribute to feelings of tiredness, lethargy, exhaustion, depression, hyperactivity, nervousness, hypertension, irrational fear, anger, hostility and aggression. The usual way of coping with these conditions is either by suppressing the symptoms with toxic drugs, taking expensive therapy sessions to rationalise the experiences, turning to spiritual guidance for emotional release, or by simply resigning oneself to a life of unhappiness and lack of fulfilment. While each of these options (except the last one) can have its place within the overall task of solving life's difficulties, working on the physical environment at home can directly remove some of the causes of the problems. The changes that you make to your home therefore will not sabotage the benefits you may get from counsellors, doctors, church ministers or other spiritual advisors.

Once we have removed the features of our home that contributed to disharmony, it is time to take positive steps to create a home that is physically in harmony with our true needs and desires. This means looking at the array of colours, images, materials, plants, books etc., which we choose to have around us, as well as the way we arrange and organise them.

To define exactly what to do, we shall be tapping into knowledge both very modern and very ancient. There is an enormous amount of scientific research into the psychological effects that various environmental factors can have – for example lighting, colours and styles. There is also a huge amount of data on the physiological effects of toxic chemicals emanating from common household products. We will be looking at the most important of these and suggesting alternatives. But a significant proportion of the ideas in this book for creating more harmony in the home come from the ancient Chinese system of environment design known as 'feng shui', which is described in the next chapter.

There are many suggestions throughout this book for further reading or study, as well as recommendations of particular types of products and services that can support your home-harmonising process. To obtain more detailed information on these, see Where can I find ...? (page 128). Where more information can be obtained in this way the text is marked with this symbol – (@).

CHAPTER TWO

Feng shui

I believe that the best way to approach this subject is by giving answers to some of the most commonly asked questions:

WHAT IS FENG SHUI?

Feng shui is a system of life analysis and harmonising techniques, which use your living or working environments as physical tools, models or templates for moulding or stimulating the quality of life experience you desire. Feng shui is more than a purely subjective art, but it is not an exact science either. To create a home that is in harmony with your needs and objectives, feng shui concepts provide important guidelines.

WHERE DID IT COME FROM?

The techniques evolved over many centuries from accumulated observations and analyses of how humans interact with their environment. Although most cultures appear to have evolved some feng shui-type systems, the most comprehensive was developed in ancient China. Thus much of the terminology and the symbols commonly used have a distinct Oriental flavour. While the basic ideas in feng shui seem to be based on good common sense and sound psychology, in the last two or three hundred years there has been a tendency to shroud them in a blanket of mysticism and dogma which has made feng shui seem mysterious and fearful to some, and a religious threat to others.

HOW IS IT USED TODAY?

In the Far East, feng shui remains an important part of every-day life at home and at work. People readily follow the rules prescribed by their local tradition, family or feng shui master. Interest in this subject is now increasing in the West, and is employed in all sizes of homes and businesses. It is important to understand however that much of the traditional Oriental terminology and symbolism needs to be adapted or translated into what is meaningful to modern Western-style cultures, otherwise it can sound like pure superstition, or at best seem irrelevant.

HOW DOES IT WORK?

Feng Shui principles are used to create a relationship between the physical environment and your desires, goals and ambitions. By carefully selecting, or by making very specific changes to your living or work space, you can stimulate your subconscious mind to make all of your actions consistent with your real intentions. In this way your dreams are far more likely to come true. It's not magic – but sometimes it seems like it!

IS IT VERY HARD TO LEARN AND USE?

As with any skill or area of study, you can start making changes in your life with some basic ideas which are easy to follow and implement. You can then continue learning new techniques, methods and principles forever.

WHAT INFORMATION IS INVOLVED?

Feng Shui is a holistic subject – there is a wide range of factors to consider. These may include certain characteristics of the area in which your house or work place is located, specific features of the site and of the building's shape, configuration, interior design, the activities that it is used for, and its history. Equally important are your personal characteristics and your issues, problems, aspirations and needs.

HOW CAN I LEARN MORE ABOUT FENG SHUI?

1 Attend study courses or workshops, but remain open-minded about what you may be taught. There are many 'schools' of feng shui which often contradict each other. This is because they may have originated in different climatic conditions, cultural mores, etc., resulting in different rules for what creates a harmonious environment. It is necessary to look at what is behind any unexplained rules or dogmas, otherwise you will not be able to apply the underlying principles effectively. (@)
2 Read as many books as possible on feng shui, interior design, architecture, behavioural psychology, the principles of Taoism and other primal philosophies, Oriental medicine, macrobiotics, etc. Again, keep an open mind. (@)
3 Arrange for a professional consultation at your home or work place, and ask as many questions about the process as you can. (@)
4 Begin to use the ideas and concepts in your own environment and observe what happens. Also look at what is happening with other people in their environment.

In this little book it is not feasible or indeed necessary to describe all of the ideas and concepts of feng shui, since there are so many of them and they can become very involved and complicated. I will however describe some of the most practical and relevant in terms of harmonising your home. I group these elements of feng shui under the headings of principles, models and tools.

PRINCIPLE ONE – THE MATERIAL ENVIRONMENT INFLUENCES THOUGHTS

People who look or feel happier tend to be more successful in life

You may have noticed that if you are feeling quite happy, but are then forced to stay for any length of time in a dark, crowded or untidy space, you will gradually begin to feel depressed and your thoughts will become more negative. Similarly, if you are anxious or depressed while designing or decorating or even choosing a home, the chances are that you will select a design that reflects your mood or your fear at that time. The problem now will be that every day your home will reinforce the feelings you had when you chose, designed or decorated it. It will then become very difficult to change your habitual thought patterns and move to more positive ones. We know that people who look or feel happier tend to be more successful in life, so by surrounding yourself with negative patterns you may end up feeling thoroughly disenchanted and rejected as well. This lowers your energy still further and the cycle of decline continues.

This principle can be used in reverse – that is: start to harmonise your home following the simple guidelines in this book, and in response your thought patterns and beliefs will start to become more positive and soon you will expect your life generally to be more harmonious, and the Universe will have no option but to acquiesce to your new belief – if you let it!

PRINCIPLE TWO – THE 'ENERGY' OF A SPACE

Our overall experience of a space, whether indoors or outside, is a combination of our interpretation of all that our senses pick up – light, heat, sound, temperature, smell, texture, shape etc. This combination of various forms or energy is call 'chi' (pronounced chee) and every environment has its own special chi. We, as individuals also have a personal chi that includes factors such as vitality, temperament, appearance, and so on. Since we are all different, the effect on our personal chi, of the chi of any particular environment will also be different. However, environments, or particular features of an environment, can be said to have good chi or bad chi depending on how it affects the average person.

Although you may not have heard it expressed in this way before, you are already well aware of this phenomenon. You know that some places feel better than others although you may not always be able to pin-point exactly what it is that is creating the difference. Feng shui helps to identify these factors so that you can do something about them in your own home if necessary.

An environment with good chi feels, to most people, comfortable, supportive, pleasing and harmonious – the kind of place that immediately makes you feel welcome and which you don't want to leave. Our objective is to make our homes like this. Of course there is no absolute quantification of chi. Our actual

What represents harmony and good chi for a bedroom, may differ from the harmony and good chi appropriate for a living room

experience of a space will depend on our own varying chi and the environmental variables such as light, weather, season, temperature etc. The idea however is to create a home that satisfies most people, most of the time.

One more point about chi. Different parts of a home have different functions, so what represents harmony and good chi for a bedroom, may differ from the harmony and good chi appropriate for a living room or kitchen.

MODEL ONE – YIN AND YANG

Yin and yang represent relative qualities of different aspects of energy. For example, when considering energy in the form of light, bright light is considered to be yang, darkness is yin. Twilight is more yang than darkness, but more yin than full daylight. Below is a list of the relative yin and yang qualities for other aspects of energy.

YIN	YANG
cold	hot
still/calm	moving/active
relaxing	energising
descending	rising
curved shapes	angular shapes
quiet	noisy
plain and simple	complex and cluttered
soft	hard
light	heavy
weak	strong
dark	bright
no contrast	high contrast

violet indigo blue green yellow orange red

Feng shui uses this model to maintain a balance within the home and between the home and yourself. For example, if your home does not have many windows or receives little direct sunlight and you persistently feel tired (i.e. it is very yin in this respect), then you would compensate for this by adding more yang characteristics, such as artificial lighting or objects that move, to create a more energising environment. If your life seems very complex and hectic and you find it hard to relax, (i.e. your life style may be too yang), then it is advisable to create a more yin environment with soft furnishings, simple decor and quiet colours.

Moderation in all things is the message, and the yin/yang theory will help you to find it

The best approach for creating harmony using yin/yang principles is to start by making the basic features relatively yin (soft, plain-coloured walls, minimum clutter, etc.) then add yang elements such as bright pictures, plants, coloured lamps and so on, until you feel that the correct balance has been reached. In this way it is easier to energise or calm a space by simply adding or removing things. Bear in mind also that rooms allocated to rest and relaxation, like bedrooms, should be more yin than working areas such as a kitchen.

One other point is that going to the extremes of either yin or yang conditions leads to the exact opposite. For example, if your life style is hectic, your home noisy, cluttered and painted in strong, bright colours, you live a very yang life. Chances are that you will soon become exhausted and ill – which is an extreme yin condition. Moderation in all things is the message, and the yin/yang theory will help you to find it.

MODEL TWO – ARCHETYPAL ENERGIES

One of the most intriguing concepts in feng shui is that of energy or chi archetypes. There are two primary archetypal systems, one with five archetypes (see The five elements model, page 17) and the other with nine (see The ba-gua model, page 14). The two systems are closely related.

Each element of the 'nine archetypes' system (often refered to as the ba-gua or pa-qua system) is defined by a Chinese name and a symbol, but we will simply refer to them by their numbers – one to nine. Each of these is associated with several different factors including personality and character types based on your birthday (rather like Western astrology (@)), a compass direction, organs of the body, specific colours and the essence of a characteristic feature of the natural environment (wind = invisible, penetrating power; water = flexible, adaptable, deep; earth = firm, nurturing, central etc.). The archetypes are also associated with nine primary aspects of human life as shown in the ba-gua model (figure 2-1). The relationship between your personality number and year of birth is shown in Appendix 1 (see page 131). To use this model in its entirety is far too complex for the purposes of this book, but we will use a couple of aspects of it for associating areas of the home with particular aspects of life in Model Three – the ba-gua system for spaces (see page 18).

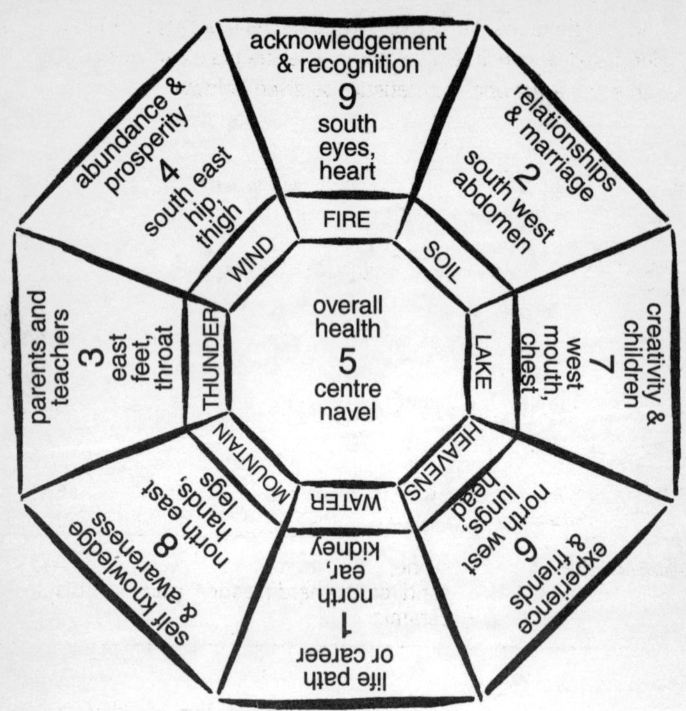

Figure 2-1 The Ba-Gua System of Archetypal 'Energies'

The five elements model condenses the nine energy archetypes described above into five primary 'elements', each of which carries an array of characteristics as given below:-

Element name	FIRE	EARTH	METAL	WATER	WOOD
Character numbers	9	2, 5, 8	6, 7	1	3, 4
Symbolic shape	pointed	flat	dome	wavy	tall & slim
Typical movement	expanding & contracting	converging	condensing	flowing	upward & outward
Colours	red/ purple	yellow/ brown	white/ grey	blue/ black	green/ jade
Materials	fire	stone, sand, earth, ceramic	metal, hard plastic	water, glass	wood, plants

Some typical characteristics of environments dominated by one of these elements are as follows:

Fire Very energetic, and lively. Great environments for stimulating activity but not appropriate for concentration or relaxation.

Earth Places where people tend to gather, and where fundamentals of problems or activities can be seen more clearly. Gives a sense of support but in excess can feel restrictive and obstructive.

Metal Rather cold and rigid, but can be good for getting down to work and focusing on specific things for sharp, quick results. Can be striking to look at but tend not to be particularly relaxing.

Water Cool and flexible. Ideas can flow easily and deep emotions can be explored. Not appropriate where stability is a key issue.

Wood Places for starting new projects, generating new ways of doing things, growth or recuperation from illness. Quite calming and therefore good for the routine aspects of activities and managing projects.

In feng shui, the environment is said to be balanced when the characteristics of each of these elements are present in one form or another in fairly even proportions. So for example, the earth element may be represented by a beige carpet or large ceramic pot; wood could be in the form of plants or natural wooden furniture; metal is usually represented by a white ceiling, but can also be in dome-topped clocks or mirrors; water can be seen in a fish tank, fountain or even a picture or flowing patterns on curtains; fire can be a real fire or lighted candles, or anything bright red or orange in colour. The proportions of the elements in each space may be harmonised to the activities intended for it. If you need to be especially creative and have ideas flow easily, try using more blues and greens or hang a picture of a river flowing through an arboreal landscape. If you lack energy, light some candles, add red objects to your space or hang a picture of red, pointed roof tops or spires for example. Simply use your imagination to create the balance you need in any particular room, and let your subconscious mind do the rest for you.

If you need to be especially creative and have ideas flow easily, try using more blues and greens

In addition to the basic energy archetype of each of these elements, there is another effect created by the relationships between them. The primary energetic relationships are shown in the following diagram:

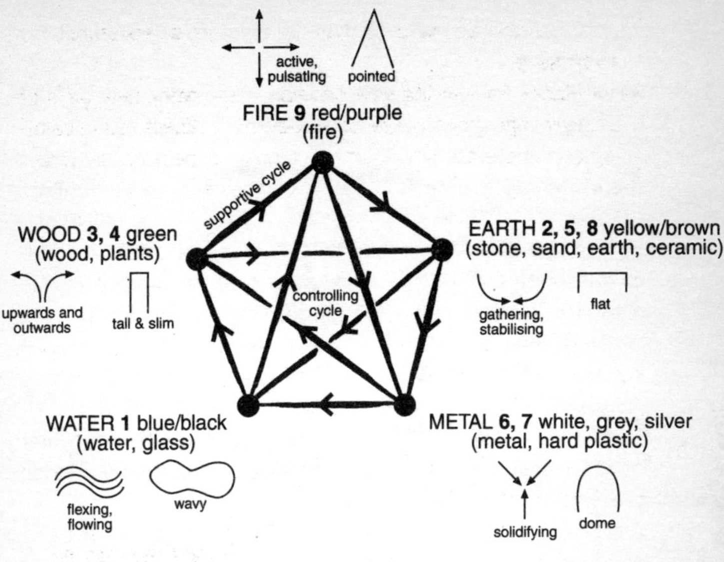

Figure 2-2 The five elements system of archetypal 'energies'

Two kinds of relationship are shown; supportive and controlling. In the supportive relationships, the characteristics of one element are enhanced or supported by the characteristics of the preceding one. Thus 'earth'- type energies are reinforced by 'fire'- type energies. If you need to enhance 'earth' in your environment (for example you may feel the need for more nurturing or stability in your life), then in addition to having more 'earth'-related colours, materials shapes, etc., add a little 'fire' in the form of red things, candles, and so on. But don't overdo it – if 'fire' is too strong and does not respect the characteristics of 'earth', it has the opposite effect and you will feel smothered and entrapped. You can use these relationships in reverse as well. So if there is too much 'fire' in your life (say you are hyperactive, surrounded by noise, and have lots of red things around you, and have a partner with a natal birth number of nine) you can reduce the stress of all this by increasing the 'earth' characteristics of your space, since 'earth' feeds off or drains 'fire' energies.

In the controlling relationships, the characteristics of one element are influenced by those opposite them. This influence is subtly different from the supportive relationship. Here, a little 'fire' can have a stimulating effect on 'metal' environments or personal situations. Excessive 'fire' however, dominates and oppresses 'metal' which can lead to a lack of focus or insufficient attention to the details in the home and in your life in general. If you have too much 'fire' in your life and environment (as described in the paragraph above) you can suppress the effects by adding 'water' characteristics (i.e. real water or blues and blacks to your surroundings). This can however create a sense of great tension if done to excess. This is acceptable if you want to make a quick, clear and decisive change in your life, but it will be difficult to tolerate and be quite exhausting over extended periods.

MODEL THREE – THE BA-GUA SYSTEM FOR SPACES

Another method of harmonising your home with your personal strengths or aspirations is to assign the nine specific aspects of life defined at the beginning of model two to specific areas of the home. There are several established ways of doing this, most of which use the compass directions to define which areas should be associated with which of the nine aspects of life. Such methods however seem to have evolved at a time when people tended to live in individual, detached houses with fairly simple shapes, and when the life style was far more influenced by the sun and seasons than many life styles today. Another approach, which is more practical for most modern living conditions, uses the entrance to a space, rather than compass directions, as the reference point for allocating areas to the nine aspects of life. This model works as follows:

1 Draw a plan of your plot of land, house, flat, or room, placing the main entrance at the bottom of the page. (If you live in a flat, the entrance we are interested in is the one to your personal space, not the communal entrance.)

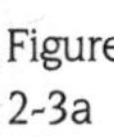

Figure 2-3a

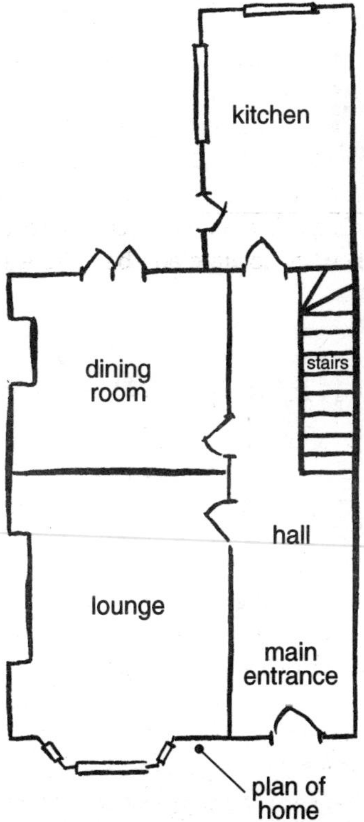

2 Divide the area used by your land, house, flat or room into nine equal parts.

Figure 2-3b

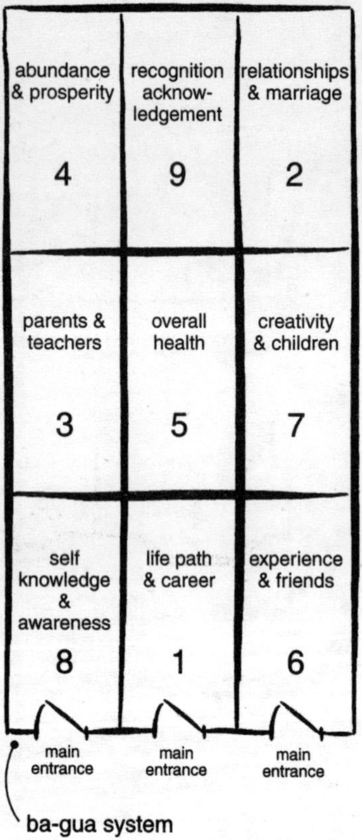

3 Mark in each part, a specific aspect of life in accordance with the examples below.

Figure 2-3c

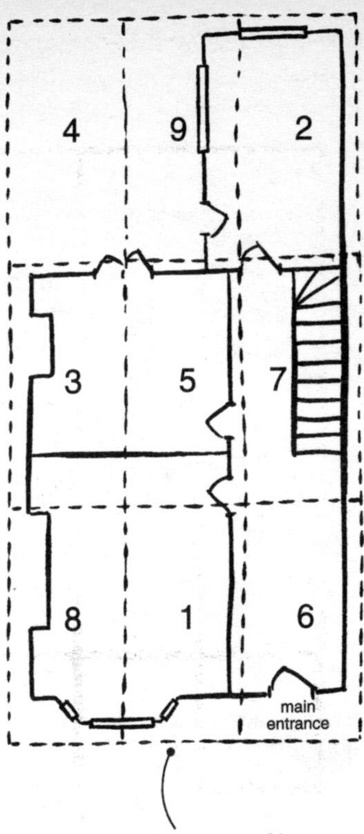

Note that:

- The direction in which you mainly enter your land, home or room should be the same as if entering any of the three bottom ba-gua elements (i.e. 'self knowledge and awareness', 'career and path', or 'experience and helpers'.)
- If part of the ba-gua lies outside of the area of your land, home or room, that part is said to be missing from your space and various corrections may need to be made within your home to create the effect of a more regular shape. (See chapter five.)
- The ba-gua can be used simultaneously on your plot of land,

your house and on individual rooms if required.

- If your home has more than one storey, the upper floors can be treated in two different ways depending on how you use those storeys. If, as in many family houses, the upper floor is primarily bedrooms and is not really lived in during the day, then treat each room as a separate space using the ba-gua on that space as described above. If your upper floor(s) has multiple uses day and night, then place the ba-gua over a plan of the whole floor, but bear in mind that the direction in which you enter that space may not be the same as the direction in which you enter the house (for example, if the stairs to the upper floor make a right angle turn).
- Small exclusions or projections from the main body of the land, home or room, do not affect the positioning of the ba-gua.

Now you have a model for associating the main aspects of life with particular spaces within the home, room and/or plot of land, and you can use this to help harmonise your home with a specific change that you wish to make in your life. If, for example you were concerned about your level of prosperity, you should start working on the rear, left corner of your land, home and/or room. If your finances are in a mess, make sure that this area is made as clean and tidy as possible. If your finances are healthy and you want them to stay that way, place something solid-looking in that area (symbolically stabilising the situation). If you find it hard to create prosperity in your life, you may need to energise that space by adding light, objects with moving elements (fish in a tank, clock with a second hand), bright red or orange decorative items, a multi-faceted refracting glass ball hanging in a window to catch sunlight, or anything else that for you represents the idea of wealth and prosperity.

But this is only half of the job. You must also address the diagonally opposite corner:–

- 'Experience and helpers'. Taoist philosophy (and that of most religions as well) suggests that you receive back in one form or another what you give away. So if prosperity is an issue for you, it is also necessary to consider what level of prosperity you are helping others to achieve, or what kind of support you are offering to the community around you. To enhance your awareness of this aspect of life you need to do the same clearing, cleaning and energising actions in the front, right corner of the home as you did for the rear, left corner.

In this way you have used your home to symbolically create harmony and balance in the flow of prosperity and support in your life. You can follow the same approach to deal with any other issues in your life, and always remember to think about the aspect which is opposite to the one that primarily concerns you, so:

- for 'relationships and marriage', work also on 'self knowledge and awareness'. (It is hard to have caring relationships with others before you have an equivalent relationship with yourself, and vice versa.)
- for 'creativity and children' issues, work also on 'parents and teachers'. (By resolving any issues around those that influenced you in the past, you can free up your mind to be creative in your own way now and in the future.)
- for 'recognition and acknowledgement' work also on 'career and path'. (Recognition is a natural by-product of doing what you are best suited to and where you feel that you can contribute most to society. This could be in your job or it could be bringing up your children responsibly. Acknowledgement also brightens the path we are taking even further.)

The following chapters give a number of other examples of how to use this ba-gua model in different situations.

TOOLS

Tools are the items that you can add to your environment to create specific effects. There are many such tools mentioned in the rest of the book, but below is a summary of those that you will probably find most useful (@):

Tools are the items that you can add to your environment to create specific effects.

To make a space seem larger (@)

- large mirrors
- bright, landscape pictures
- extra lighting

To make a space seem taller (@)

- up-lighters
- tall plants
- tall, slim design features or objects

To energise an environment (@)

- moving objects (fish, clocks with a pendulum or a second hand, etc.)
- extra lights
- refracting glass balls (if direct sunlight is available)
- brightly coloured or shiny objects and pictures
- vigorous, bright plants
- wind chimes (if exposed to a draft)
- mirrors (carefully placed)
- bird feeders or bird baths (for the garden)
- mobiles or windmills

To stabilise existing conditions (@)

- heavy stones or rocks
- heavy or large furniture
- large, solid statues

To improve air quality (@)

- plants (see chapters nine and ten)
- ionisers
- natural deodorisers and scents (see chapter ten)

This completes our very brief overview of some basic concepts in feng shui. Although there is a lot more to learn, you already have enough information to get you moving in the right direction. (@) The following chapters will give you lots of ideas on how to improve your environment by using feng shui, but one of the most effective and easiest steps is described in the next chapter – Making space.

CHAPTER THREE

Making space

Whenever we want to do anything we must make space for it. To make a cake we must clear the kitchen work surface of items that would get in the way; to put new plants in the garden we must clear away weeds and other debris first; to think up a new plan or start a new project we need to clear our mind of other issues. So it is with creating more harmony in your home. Step one is getting rid of blockages and obstructions to harmony. These come in many guises, which can be summarised as clutter, incompletions, ergonomic and energy blocks.

If you deal properly with these issues, you will be amazed at how much space you create in your home, so that further steps will seem, and in fact will be, so much easier. You will also be amazed at how much space you create in your mind. You will feel lighter and more energetic and will start to bubble with new ideas and solutions to problems that may have bothered you for years. What's more, getting rid of blockages and obstructions costs very little or no money at all – you may even make money.

> *Step one is getting rid of blockages and obstructions to harmony*

What it does cost however is WILL POWER. Taking this first step is physically quite easy in most cases, but it can be emotionally very hard indeed. We need to confront the fear of letting go of old habits, beliefs and attitudes which are bound up in the things we collect around us and in the way we have positioned them in our homes. Let us begin with clutter.

Confront the fear of letting go of old habits, beliefs and attitudes

CLUTTER IS...

RUBBISH

Old newspapers, magazines, beer bottles, empty bags, time-expired food, ballpoint pens with no ink left, unused boxes and other unusable and worn-out items. Rubbish is found in the main part of the house, sometimes on the floor for all to see, sometimes in the back of cupboards, which have not been opened for years. Rubbish is often found in the attic, the shed, garden or garage. No excuses! Get rid of it! NOW! Before reading on.

Old things that you used in the past but don't use now (I am referring to inanimate objects, of course, not other members of the family!). These include:

CLOTHES

Old styles, worn out, misshapen, jackets beyond repair, trousers, dresses, shirts, underwear, socks, shoes, ties, hats – all stuffed into wardrobes, cupboards and drawers, unused year after year. So some things may remind you of that special night, that great holiday or how you were in your prime, but that was then, and this is now. You want more harmony now. You may tell yourself that you want to keep something for working in the garden or for wearing indoors in cold weather – who are you kidding? Come on, be brave, and chuck them out. (I had to get my girlfriend to purge my wardrobes as it was far too traumatic a task for me alone.)

BOOKS

This is another common form of clutter from past usage. Unlike old clothes however, books are often on display so that you see them day after day. If you have been bookish for a number of years the book shelves can get so full they may even be bending under the weight. The symbolism you create here is that your mind is also stuffed full to the point that you can hardly cope with the demands on your time, and that there is no room for anything new in your life. No room in fact for things that may be more harmonious with what is happening now and who you are being now. So have a good look at all those books. Some may contain useful reference material and some may be especially inspiring, many however, you know that you will never look at again. I recommend a three stage process for dealing with a surfeit of books.

Stage one – pull out and immediately discard insignificant novels, irrelevant textbooks, out-of-date travel guides, Christmas annuals and humorous books that you no longer find funny.

Stage two – pull out books that you think you probably should discard, but are really reluctant to part company with, and put them in a box. Then put that box away somewhere inconspicuous for six months or a year. If you do not miss those books at all during this time it is probably safe to give them away or sell them.

Stage three – take the reference books that you may occasionally use, such as The Home Repair Manual, the English/Russian dictionary, *Karma Sutra*, The Dinner Party Cook Book, etc., and put them away in a cupboard out of sight. What you are left with on the shelves is an array of useful and inspirational books, and lots of open space for new ideas and possibilities.

TOOLS AND UTENSILS

Have you noticed how DIY tools and kitchen utensils, pots and pans etc., seem to breed in the darker recesses of cupboards and drawers? And where do those disembodied handles and odd lids from non-existent containers come from? All of them are leftovers from past lives and past projects. They must go, along with odd bits of cutlery and crockery, half-empty tubs of dried up putty, glue and paint. Keep one clean, working or usable item of each type and perhaps one spare that you will definitely need, and then get rid of the remainder.

JUNK

You will probably find most of this in the attic, cellar, garage/shed or down the alley by the side of the house where even the cat fears to tread. Junk is so unbelievably useless it is in danger of becoming a new art form. Little Johnny, who is now twenty-five, weighs fifteen stone and plays rugby for Newcastle is not going to need his rusty kiddies' tricycle any more! And that jemmy, crowbar and pick-axe handle in the corner of the shed – throw them out. Forget the sentimental value, even if they did belong to your granny.

REALLY USELESS ITEMS

These are things that you bought or were given and have served no useful purpose whatsoever. Quite often these are impulse-bought souvenirs or token gifts from remote relatives such as the little china clay dog (now chipped) on the window-sill that Auntie Flo brought you from her trip to the seaside in 1976. There may be a cute little glass jar you picked up at a jumble sale years ago, but you are not sure why, or what to do with it now. All these things block your space, block your creativity and your capacity to harmonise your home. Either sell them or give them away.

BROKEN OR DAMAGED THINGS

It is tempting to put off repairing or discarding items that are damaged in the normal course of life. But this is like putting off or avoiding the creation of harmony in your home and is subconsciously quite destructive, especially if what is broken can be repaired easily or is very cheap to replace. For example, I know of people who keep using chipped, cracked or scratched crockery year after year despite having perfectly good crockery shut away in bedroom cupboards. The message they reinforce in themselves each day is 'I don't deserve harmony in my daily life'. Other common examples of this type are clocks with flat batteries or broken springs, blown light bulbs, holes in socks, loose saucepan handles, sticking door locks, squeaking gate and door hinges and furniture that has come unglued. You can probably find more examples in your own home.

Don't waste money on repairing items that you seriously plan to replace in a reasonably short time

Sometimes repairs and replacements for washing machines, window panes and so on, can be more expensive. If you have the money, 'bite the bullet' and get them fixed as soon as possible. If you feel that you don't have the money at the moment make a firm savings plan to tackle one repair project at a time. (@)

One last point on broken and damaged things concerns pragmatism. Don't waste money on repairing items that you seriously plan to replace in a reasonably short time. In my house for example, I will not bother to replace a cracked window-pane in the front door because the whole door is to be replaced next month.

INCOMPLETIONS

Projects that we began and never finished are incompletions. They distract us from critical work or other activities and thus are a serious obstruction to creative harmony. Some typical incompletions I have seen recently include a half-built front garden wall (no progress in six months), an unfinished home-built loudspeaker kit (no progress in ten years!), a half-redecorated bedroom (three months overdue), two years' worth of unfiled receipts and invoices from a small retail business, three days' worth of dirty dishes in the sink and a half-knitted pullover that has been waiting to be finished for over a year. Quite often, incompletions occur in our homes because we take on too many projects at once, we then get confused as to how best to utilise time, which leads to anxiety, which leads to exhaustion, which creates yet more incompletions. Also, incompletions on the physical plane are likely to be mirrored by incompletions on the mental plane such as unresolved relationship issues, lack of clarity about career goals, unsettled arguments with relatives, friends or neighbours.

Since mental plane incompletions can be very difficult and stressful to resolve, it is better to create more emotional space by dealing with physical plane incompletions first – these being relatively simple, though not always easy.

If you feel overloaded with incompletions, add another list to your harmonisation plan: repairs and replacements. Make a list of incomplete projects, estimate what it will take (time and/or money) to finish them, decide which ones are not worthwhile, prioritise the remainder and make a clear, realistic plan for their completion, i.e. one at a time.

Incompletions on the physical plane are likely to be mirrored by incompletions on the mental plane

ERGONOMIC BLOCKAGES

Have you ever been in a house where the path from the settee in the living room to the fridge in the kitchen could easily be part of a marine commando assault training course? First you struggle to get out of the settee which is far too soft to provide proper support, and immediately bang your knee on the nested side tables. You now have two choices for getting to the door to the hallway: a) the fireplace route – where the knife-like edge of a glass-topped coffee table presses you perilously close to the television and red hot gas fire; or b) the drinks cabinet route – where you must gingerly manoeuvre around the Victorian standard lamp and the armchair, without knocking over the large vase of artificial roses perched dangerously on top of the bureau. If you make it to the hall door safely, further surprises await you. Mind that little telephone table just around the corner but don't stub your toes on the umbrella stand opposite! Now, however, the kitchen door is in sight and you make a run for it, knocking over the three empty milk bottles left in the hall and squashing little Jennifer's Barbie doll lying in the middle of the floor. Eventually you burst through into the kitchen hitting your head on the plate rack and getting impaled on the sharp corner of the kitchen table. Just when you think it is safe to approach the fridge, you are petrified by an unearthly wail from the cat that you have just trodden on.

Lots of blockages and obstructions to freedom and movement create stress and disharmony in the home.

Lots of blockages and obstructions to freedom and movement create stress and disharmony in the home. Physical harmony, as in musical harmony, allows natural and easy transition from one part to another. I frequently find that people living in houses with many such obstructions, find other aspects of their lives rather blocked too. Maybe at work or in their creative endeavours. There always seems to be something standing in the way of progress. What other kinds of situations in the home are representative of obstructions in our lives? Check your home for these symptoms:

- Walking into one or more of your main rooms, you are immediately confronted by some piece of furniture, which forces you to make a sharp change of direction or which creates a visual wall or barrier.
- Frequently used narrow spaces such as halls and landings, which have too many items of furniture or decorative pieces in them, creating an even more constricted channel.
- Having pieces of furniture that are too large for the room – the room appears overloaded or totally dominated by the cupboards, tables, chairs etc. The effect is worse if the furniture is dark. Large plants can also create a sense of domination and obstruction, especially if they reach the ceiling. The symbolism here is that no more growth or progress is possible, which is not a very positive message for your unconscious mind.
- Very low hanging lamps positioned over areas where you need to walk.
- Lots of smaller things scattered over the floor such as side tables, books, papers, toys, clothes, boxes etc.
- Low archways leading from one room to the next.
- Walls directly behind doors, so that when you walk into a house or room you are immediately confronted by a wall. (In such cases, put a large flat or convex mirror – one that curves outwards – on the wall to create an impression of depth.)
- Doors that open towards the centre of a room rather than against a wall (a common feature in British houses).
- A kitchen with an 'island' in the centre containing a sink or cooker. Unless the kitchen is very large, this can feel like an obstruction to free movement.

More subtle blockages restrict your view of the world, and this can be reflected in a limited outlook on your life in general. Such restrictions include low-hanging curtains that block the view from inside, and large trees, walls or buildings just outside the main front or back windows of your home.

The point is to do the best that you can with the ideas given in this and other chapters in the book

Having identified the main physical blockages to harmonious energy flows in your home, it is necessary to figure out what to do about them. I will assume that major rebuilding work is not feasible for you at the moment or that you cannot immediately replace or dispose of large pieces of furniture that you may now see as a potential cause of problems. If, however, you can do these things, then I encourage you to do so as soon as possible. For the rest of us, here are some solutions to giving your home an enema treatment.

Firstly, if you have conscientiously completed the de-cluttering process described in the first part of this chapter you may find that you don't need so many cupboards and drawers. If so, remove some of them from your space. You may also be prompted to question whether other pieces of furniture are really worth the space they take up.

Secondly, look at the arrangement of the furniture that is left. Can you clear all doorways of obstructions and create an easy path through the room? Many houses have small rooms and sometimes a bed alone can virtually fill a bedroom, but the point is to do the best that you can with the ideas given in this and other chapters in the book. If possible, it is best to arrange a room so that the centre is clear of any furniture or other obstruction. This is especially important for rooms where people naturally tend to congregate or relax – such as the kitchen or the lounge. As you change the layout of your rooms, do remember that things must be placed in a way that is still practical, accessible or functional. Also understand that an alteration that creates more space for you may seem strange, even awkward at first, although in many cases the improvement is so obvious you will wonder why you didn't do it before. Allow yourself a few weeks to see how the new arrangement works for you, before reconsidering.

It is now time to look at other, perhaps smaller changes, such as raising low-hanging curtains or lamps if necessary. Also consider pruning overgrown trees or bushes that may be blocking your view from the windows. You can make narrow spaces, like some hallways, appear more spacious by having plenty of light in the room and bright landscape pictures or a large mirror on the wall (the mirror should be in a frame or at least bevel edged). However it is not recommended to have large mirrors in the bedroom or in areas that you have not cleared up and organised first. In this latter case, your subconscious sees double the amount of work to do, and that can contribute to a sense of being overwhelmed.

If you have been able to use the suggestions in this chapter you will already be experiencing a new feeling of freedom and ease in your home. You will start to see it in a new light; as a tool for creating harmony and change in your inner as well as your outer life.

The best time to observe the reactions you are having to the appearance of your home is as you enter it and leave it. First and last impressions are the subject of the next chapter.

CHAPTER FOUR

First and lasting impressions

When we meet someone, our minds go through a very quick analysis to evaluate and categorise that person. Whatever our minds decide about the person at that moment can stick with us for a very long time, and influence how we behave in subsequent interactions.

A similar process occurs when we view our homes (and anything else for that matter) after we have been away from it for a time. If, when you approach your home after a day at work or after going shopping and you see a broken gate, flaking paintwork or an untidy garden, the impression is of something run down or neglected and definitely not harmonious. But this is your home and as we said earlier, this is an extension or reflection of yourself and the attitudes and beliefs that you might have had in the past. However, the idea of 'run down and neglected' you unconsciously assign to yourself now and this becomes how you feel and eventually how you are, and this in turn affects what you do inside the home. So if you would rather be more alive, energetic, elegant and in harmony with the world in general, a very good place to start is by harmonising the parts of your home environment that provide us with first impressions. The key areas for this are: the external front aspect of the home, the main entrance area and hallway, the bedroom (the first space you see after being asleep and away in your dreams), and the bathroom (the first place where you are likely to see yourself and be fully conscious of a new day).

Last impressions of a place are as important as first impressions. An example of this is those shops that you visited once, but never felt inclined to go back to – you were left with an impression that they were not comfortable or supportive.

If your home looks a mess when you leave it behind, you tend to carry the idea with you into the outside world that you or your life is in an equivalent mess. This is all in your subconscious and while, on the surface, you think that you are behaving independently of the home situation, there will almost certainly be some aspect of your appearance, body language or manner that betrays the real state of affairs. Others will pick up these little messages (also mostly unconsciously), and react to you accordingly. So a more harmonious home can also lead to a more harmonious and successful relationship with the world outside.

Even more important however is the world inside – that is the world inside your mind. The impression of yourself that you take to bed with you has deep and far reaching effects on your health, prosperity, relationships and overall sense of well-being. Therefore the last places you see at night, bathroom and bedroom, are especially important and need to be 'harmonised' as soon as possible.

FRONT ASPECT

Let us begin with harmonising the front aspect of the home. This could include a grand entrance gate, a drive, front garden and porch or if you live in a block of flats, the front of your home may consist of a door in a corridor. Whatever is there, it must first be clean and tidy. Then decide if any simple repairs are necessary. Some of my recent cases include a broken gate, flaking paintwork on the front door and windows, overgrown hedge, collapsing garden wall, damaged and uneven driveway paving. Consider now if there are any features that are likely to create an unwelcoming effect. These could include lots of dead or spiky plants in the front garden or around the front door, sharply angled brick or stone borders with points facing people as they enter or leave the house, low porticoes or flower baskets hanging low over the front door. Light is very important, especially on dark winter days. One lamp over the centre of the front door or a lamp either side creates a warm and welcoming feel. Well tended and colourful plants either side of the front door also give a good impression.

Choose a colour that represents the character you wish to portray

If you live in a block of flats, you may have fewer options for 'harmonising' the entrance, but you can make sure that the front door is painted, that the bell or knocker works properly and the handle, letter box or any other features are clean and polished. It is sometimes possible to fix an extra light outside your flat or (given enough space and light) have a potted plant there. Another possibility is to place a nice mat in front of the door to act as a transition zone between the public area and your private space.

There are many different ideas about what colour a front door should be. In feng shui, certain colours are said to be representative of particular compass directions. For example north is black, east is green, south is red and west is white. Another approach suggests that your door colour should be representative of the main breadwinner of the house, in accordance with his or her birth year. Appendix 1 and figure 2-2 show the appropriate colours for people born in each year of the nine year feng shui astrological cycle (see pages 17 and 131). In yet another system, you should choose a colour that represents the character you wish to portray. In this case, black or other dark colours means quiet and introvert, bright red means lively and energetic, yellow is for those who like to have visitors, pink for those looking for love, white for formality, green for creativity, and brown or natural wood for people who wish to be seen as down-to-earth types. Finally, you can use basic yin and yang principles in accordance with the amount of natural light to which your main door is exposed. So for dark (yin) entrances – in a block of poorly lit flats, a front door behind a large dark portico or facing a space which has little or no sunlight – you should select a light, energising (yang) colour such as yellow. For yang conditions (i.e. lots of bright natural daylight), you could try stronger or darker colours. In my view there are no absolute rules on this. Choose a door colour with which you feel comfortable and which harmonises with the style of the neighbourhood, the style of your house and the amount of ambient light. Beware of colour clutter – i.e. kaleidoscopic colour schemes or colours which do not fit with the style of the house or character of the neighbourhood. (@)

A word about waste bins and bags. These of course should not be seen when entering or leaving the home except perhaps if they are put out for collection. For some homes however, there is no choice and waste must be stored in the front of the building. In such cases it may be possible to construct a wooden or brick bunker to hide the bins and bags or to plant a hedge to surround them. If neither of these options is possible then keep the waste bin clean and neat and disinfect it from time to time to reduce smells.

If there is a garden or another reasonably spacious area in front of your home, it is possible to create a harmonious design based on the five archetypal elements of feng shui as described in chapter two.

Each element could be represented by either materials, shapes or colours. For example:

Wood - plants, wooden fence and/or gate, trees.
Fire - red flowers or berries, red paintwork, red bricks or paving, 'saw tooth' arrangement of paving, lamps.
Earth - yellow flowers, stones, brown/yellow bricks or paving.
Metal - white flowers, railings, metal gate, white paintwork.
Water - blue or black paintwork, pond, bird-bath, flowing or curved shapes of flower beds, walls or pathways.

The possibilities are infinite; so aim for harmony and be creative.

MAIN ENTRANCE

Once inside your front door, there is a second chance to set the tone of your home before penetrating the inner sanctum and whatever may be lying in wait for you there. There are four primary aspects to consider in creating a harmonious entrance.

A space will seem to be larger if it is decorated in light, plain colours

SPACE

If the entrance to your home is small and narrow, it creates the idea in your subconscious mind of constriction, restriction and limitation, which then tends to be associated with 'home' in general and yourself in particular. In chapter three, we suggested several ways to make more space including removing all unnecessary pieces of furniture, raising any low-hanging lights and using a flat or convex mirror on a wall. In addition, a space will seem to be larger if it is decorated in light, plain colours.

LIGHT

A bright light in the entrance (either natural or artificial) creates a sense of warmth and invitation. Dark entrances and hallways can be interpreted as unwelcoming, blocked and even dangerous to our subconscious minds. Also, I think that this is the best area for which to invest in a really elegant lamp shade – perhaps a cut-glass shade or a mini chandelier. The idea is to encourage the image of energy, elegance and quality to greet you as you enter, and stimulate you as you depart.

TEXTURE

Excessive amounts of hard, flat surfaces (such as tiled flooring, plain plastered walls) can look very elegant, but may also feel a little cold. In contrast, thick carpeting, heavy curtains, fancy, embossed or fabric wallpaper can feel oppressive. You need to find the right balance of textures to create the image of yourself and your home that you want to project.

SMELL

One of our strongest responses to a new place comes from the sense of smell. When you walk into your house what does it smell of? Is it pleasant and fresh or musty and stale? Does it create a feeling of calm or of stimulation? If you would like to change the smell within your home, it is necessary to find out the cause and deal with that. If you want to create a new aroma in your home, one quick solution is to use aromatherapy oil. The easiest method is to buy a small evaporator, which typically consists of a night-light candle holder supporting a crucible over the candle. Put some water in the crucible along with a few drops of the aromatherapy oil. When the candle is lit the water heats up and evaporates carrying the aroma of the oil with it. Consult an aromatherapy expert to find out which oils will help you the most in alleviating your particular problem. In general the following guidelines can be followed (@):

> *One of our strongest responses to a new place comes from the sense of smell*

- Chamomile or lavender: gives an impression of serenity, stability, wholeness and balance.
- Lemon, peppermint or rosemary: for freshness, motivation, alertness, energy and drive.

BEDROOM

This is the first and last critical environment we are aware of as we move from physical consciousness to another dream-like form of consciousness. For most people it is also the single place where we spend most time and where we develop our most intimate relationships. In this space it is therefore most important to create harmony associated with quiet, inner peace and relationships. For this there are a number of key guidelines:

MINIMALISM

Minimise the number of things in a bedroom. Keep only sleeping-related or personal items there. You may have a couple of pictures, but only if they are simple, bright and cheerful or are associated with your current close relationship – for example a photo of you and your partner in a round or oval frame. A few philosophical or spiritually related items may also be appropriate, such as a book; shrine; picture or symbol of a guru or religious prophet, or angels; holy water; flowers or candles. Things that do not contribute to harmony in a bedroom include television sets, newspapers and magazines, radio and hi-fi equipment, sports gear, computers, large mirrors, work-related books and papers – in fact anything connected with the world outside you, your relationship and your god.

> ***Minimise the number of things in a bedroom***

SIMPLICITY

This follows on from minimalism, but refers to details such as plain walls rather than fancy wallpaper, and soft colours and patterns in fabrics, bed linen or curtains. Things such as dirty clothes, cosmetics and toys should be kept inside cupboards or drawers rather than on furniture surfaces or on the floor.

SOFTNESS

Softness is expressed by the colours, shapes and textures in the room. Large surface areas should be in pale, pastel colours, so that you are not distracted or over stimulated by them. Round shapes and rounded corners or edges of furniture are better than sharp corners. This also applies to any patterns in fabric or carpets. If you already have lots of furniture with sharp corners and edges in your bedroom, increase the proportion of round things such as picture frames, clocks, small mirrors, lamps, flower pots or vases.

SLEEPING AND WAKING UP

To harmonise the transition from the normal waking state to sleep, you may consider listening to quiet, elegant music, meditating or reading some inspiring philosophical or spiritual text. For me, the most harmonious way of waking up in the morning is with the emergence of dawn and sunlight. For this reason, east-facing bedrooms are particularly good provided the light is not blocked by other buildings or that the room does not overlook a noisy road or railway. If you need to use other methods for waking up like alarm clocks or clock-radios, the transition can be quite brutal. There is an alternative device called a light alarm which is a lamp that simulates dawn by gradually increasing the amount of light it emits, allowing you to become conscious gently. (@)

CHILDREN'S ROOMS

Entering a child's or teenager's bedroom can be a horrifying experience. Treading diligently over the minefield of toys, dirty clothes and magazines, you may suddenly be confronted by a huge picture of a gruesome looking creature who is apparently the latest pop idol. After this shock, you look around in despair, certain that this child will never know or understand harmony, or ever grow up to be a normal, responsible human being. The solution to this problem is however remarkably simple – keep the door shut. Pleading, begging, talking logically, demanding or getting emotional about the mess will make no difference. A young person's mind is all over the place and that's not all bad. The best service you can offer is to set an example yourself and when he or she has problems, which they inevitably will, you can explain that to help sort things out in their minds, it is best to first sort things out in their room. If nothing else works, they will eventually try your approach. In this way you keep your hair and avoid creating a confrontational relationship with them.

BATHROOM

Harmony in the bathroom follows a similar set of rules to those for the entrance hall and bedroom – keep it simple, light, clean and tidy. Although you don't want people to lock themselves in there for too long, too often, the bathroom can be a place of rest and relaxation. Give yourself a treat occasionally by running a bath with a handful of natural sea salt and a few drops of aromatherapy essential oils (lavender is good for calming you down). Light a candle and place it on the end of the tub, then lie in the bath and either meditate, read a good philosophical book or listen to a tape of some spiritual music or a guided meditation.

How you see yourself last thing at night and first thing in the morning is most important and for this, the bathroom mirror is critical. Ideally, your reflected image should appear to you as whole and intact and surrounded by lots of space, especially above your head. In this way your subconscious sees you complete, integrated, whole and unconstrained. Of course at a conscious level you may interpret what you see as tired and bedraggled, but the message to the subconscious is far more important. For this reason the bathroom mirror should be as large as possible and in one piece (not smaller mirrors fixed together). It should also be framed, or at least bevel edged, and not have a pattern etched in it that would affect your reflected image. Smoked glass or tinted mirrors reflect a dull subdued image – don't use them.

The bathroom mirror is critical

One last point on mirrors. Avoid having mirrors facing each

other on opposite walls. Feng shui principles say that this creates unnecessary stress and confusion.

Avoid having mirrors facing each other on opposite walls

If you have been able to follow the ideas in this chapter, chances are that you will begin to feel more confident and see more possibilities for creating a really harmonious home and, at the same time, your self-esteem may start to increase. To complete our sense of balance and harmony, we need to examine balance and harmony in the shapes of the spaces in which we live, and this is discussed in the next chapter.

CHAPTER FIVE

Shaping up

The shape of the spaces or buildings we inhabit can have a surprisingly significant effect on our personal chi. At a deep subconscious level, we humans feel more comfortable in spaces that are simple in shape. The problem is that our intellectual brain, which for various 'logical', economic or abstract stylistic reasons, creates for us all kinds of odd shapes to live in. Whether referring to a plot of land, a house, flat or an individual room, at some level our mind sees the space as its territory and is bothered if it cannot easily survey the whole area from one position. This anxiety then takes away some of our vitality.

A harmonious home therefore must appear to our subconscious mind at least, to be a reasonably regular shape. But what if your land, house, flat or room is an odd shape? Is it necessary to move or rebuild it? Generally, the answer is 'no'.

Logically you know that an odd-shaped house is not an actual, physical threat to survival, but the subconscious does not work on that type of logic – it is preprogrammed in a different way. But we can use this characteristic to trick the subconscious into believing it is seeing a regular shape, so that the anxious energy can be saved for more productive tasks.

There are three main approaches to symbolically squaring-off or regularising the shape of a space: partitioning, expanding and energising.

PARTITIONING

This method involves mentally dividing the space into portions which are as close as possible to a square or rectangle, and then creating ways of marking these divisions physically. Note that it is not always necessary to make a physical wall to divide up space, the subconscious is quite satisfied with symbolic partitions such as colour changes, a row of plant pots, a mobile or wind chime hanging from the ceiling. Here are some real life examples of this type of situation to give you a better idea of this method.

A triangular-shaped garden (traditionally considered as bad feng shui, probably because it feels awkward and is difficult to use efficiently).

Plant a hedge with a small gap on one side, across the garden about two thirds the distance towards the back, and arrange the flower beds along the sides of the front portion to be narrower at the back than the front. The result is that from the house the garden looks almost square.

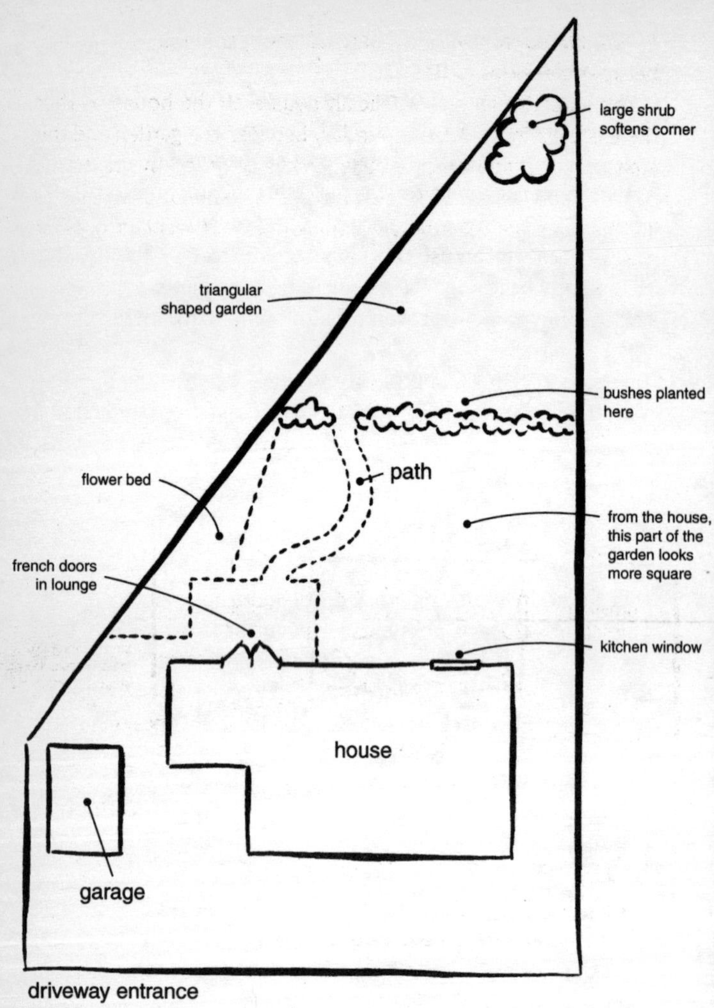

Figure 3-1 Solution for a triangular-shaped garden

A 'U'-shaped house with part of the garden in the space between the sides of the 'U'.

The objective is to symbolically square off the house so that there is a distinct straight boundary between the garden and the area to be defined as the house. This is achieved by creating a patio area in the space formed by the 'U' shape and emphasising the interface with the garden area with some plant pots or tubs.

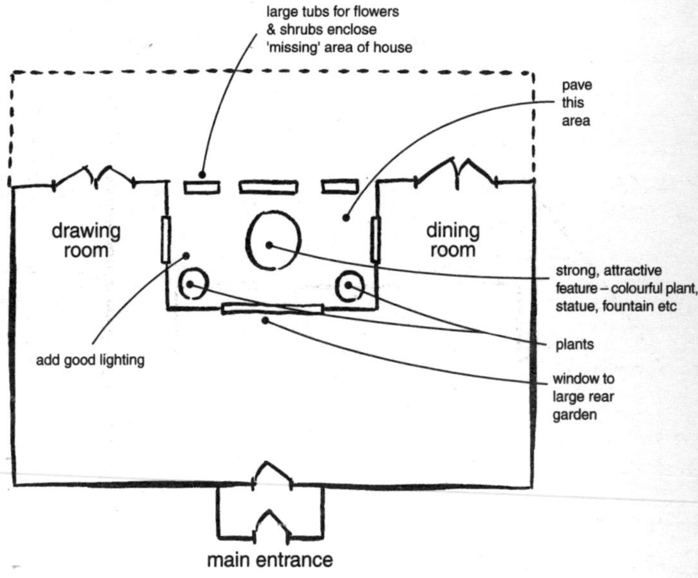

Figure 3-2 Solution for a 'U'-shaped home

An 'L'-shaped lounge/dining area.

The regularising solution is to make the smaller portion of the 'L' into the dining area and fit a brass retaining strip across the carpet where the dining area begins. Hang a mobile from the ceiling directly above the carpet-retaining strip.

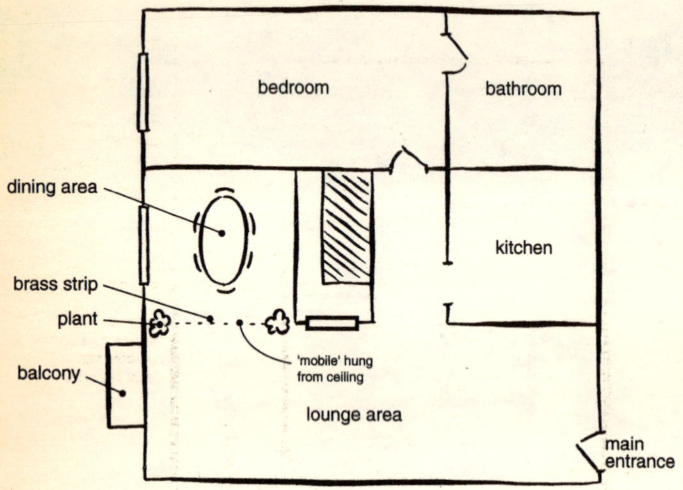

Figure 3-3 Solution for an 'L'-shaped lounge/dining room

EXPANDING

This is necessary when a wall significantly intrudes on the regular shape of a room. By placing something on this wall, the shape can be corrected, or expanded. For example, consider a room in a flat that would be square but for a large rectangular area behind which is a stairwell or lift shaft. To trick the subconscious into 'seeing' a more simple-shaped room, a mirror is placed on one of the walls of the cut out area. The mirror essentially creates the illusion of depth which, to the subconscious, makes the wall disappear. Another solution is to use a broad landscape picture with some depth in the image.

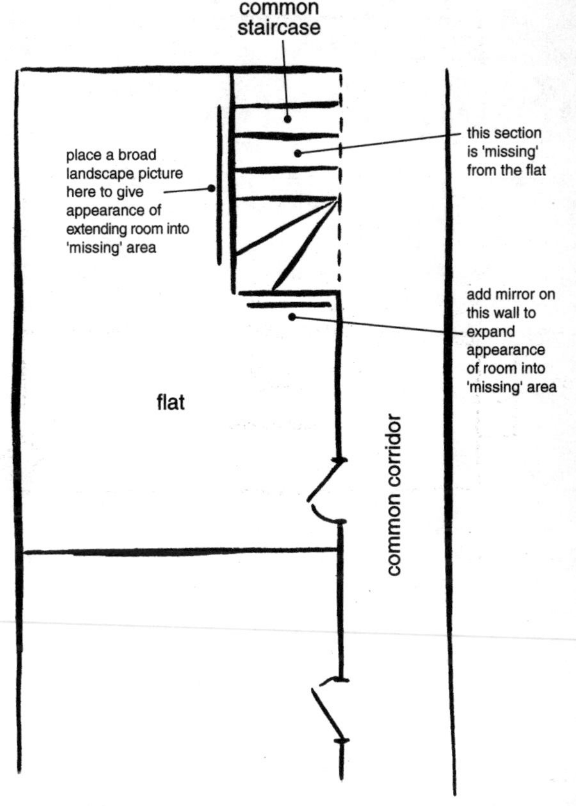

Figure 3-4 Solution for a flat with a large area cut out due to common stairwell

ENERGISING

This approach allows you to regularise an irregular-shaped space by bringing attention to the area which is physically outside it, but which needs to be included in the space to make it appear more regular in shape. For example, in the 'U'-shaped house, the central area could be made to be experienced as more of an integral part of the main house structure by putting bright lights there, creating an attractive feature such as a fountain or large tub of flowers or by using sound from a wind chime.

There are several methods and combinations of methods that can help you satisfy the subconscious mind that your land, house or room is a nice, regular shape. So take a good look at your home and determine where there are significant irregularities in the shapes. We are really only concerned here with large irregularities. Little deviations in a house or flat such as cut-outs for plumbing, shallow chimney breasts or extensions for a toilet or small utility room do not constitute major irregularities.

Another common problem with the design of houses and flats is low or sloping ceilings such as you find with rooms in a loft or attic space. In these situations, the subliminal effect can create a feeling of being oppressed or limited. Take an objective view of your home and sense whether any of the ceilings feel low or constricting. Before you do this, it is best to spend some time in other homes or buildings so that you create in your mind a reference based on how you feel elsewhere.

If you do find that your ceilings are too low, here are some suggestions for making them seem higher:

- Ensure they are clean and painted white.
- Avoid having lights that hang down from the ceiling – instead use surface-mounted lights or wall-mounted up-lighters (lamps that deflect light upwards).
- Don't paint the cornice or any trim between walls and ceiling in a darker colour.
- Use taller, slimmer versions of decorative items such as lamp

shades, plants, pictures and statues, or have vertical stripes on curtains or wallpaper.

- Choose pictures containing some direct or indirect reference to upward movement or lightness, such as tall trees, birds flying, balloons, kites, rockets, aircraft, skyscrapers.

Overhead beams can have the effect of making the ceiling appear lower and the room appear smaller. Sharp edges of beams may also absorb some of your attention and in this way drain some of your energy. Because of the association of beams with the support of great weight, it is considered very unhealthy in feng shui to sleep or sit under them – they can stimulate anxiety in the subconscious mind. Some practical ways to deal with intrusive overhead beams are:

- Paint the beams the same colour as the ceiling.
- Round-off the edges of the beams as much as possible.
- Fit spotlights or lamps on the sides of the beams.
- Fix some object which represents lightness (e.g. feather, balloon, model of a flying bird) on the beams.
- Conceal the beams behind fabric or more rigid materials such as plasterboard or hardboard.
- Move beds and chairs away from overhead beams and sloping ceilings if possible, especially if you are having difficulty sleeping or relaxing.

Rounding off corners of rooms with plants, a corner cabinet, chairs etc., or softening flower borders keeps the home in harmony with the nature from which we all have evolved

These cures are for beams which are obviously impinging on your normal field of view within the home. There is no need to become paranoid about beams or rafters if they are very high up in a loft space or very small in comparison with other structural features.

To complete our discussion on harmonising the shape and dimensions of your home it is worth remembering that the rigid box shape of most homes is a result of economical and practical construction limitations. Such structures are not found in nature however, so although the spaces of our homes should have simple shapes, this does not imply harsh, angular configurations. Rounding off corners of rooms with plants, a corner cabinet, chairs etc., or softening flower borders keeps the home in harmony with the nature from which we all have evolved.

Other characteristics of nature, colour, light and patterns are the subject of the next chapter.

CHAPTER SIX

Pattern, colour and light

The next most critical aspect of home harmonising is the energy more directly associated with light – including colours, shades, contrasts and patterns. To create a home in which the light is in harmony with the patterns and activities of daily life, we need to look again at the principles of yin and yang.

PATTERN

Patterns can be seen on walls, floors, furniture fabrics, tablecloths, vases and curtains. If the patterns are large, complex and in highly contrasting colours, then they are dynamic, and yang in nature. Small, subtle, monotonic patterns are then relatively yin. It can be difficult to relax in a space that has too many yang patterns. Victorian homes were often quite dark both in terms of the colours used and the amount and quality of available lighting – a very yin condition. Perhaps to compensate for this, patterns in furnishings, wallpapers, etc., tended to be complex and elaborate – quite yang. These extremes of yin and yang must have made the whole environment feel quite tiring.

Many modern designs go to the opposite extreme – with virtually no patterns in anything, just flat, plain surfaces, but with bright colours and lots of light. This can also be very stressful to live with. Feng shui is about finding a comfortable balance: where the basic conditions of light, colour and patterns are neutral, but with gentle tones or occasional splashes of contrasting colour and light to add interest and to harmonise with your personal taste and with what you want to do or achieve in a particular space.

The entrance to your home is a good place to set the 'tone'

Take for example, a bedroom. Here, the prime function is to provide you with the opportunity to rest, relax, recharge your biological 'batteries', make connections with your higher or spiritual nature and develop intimate relationships. These needs are all to do with calmness and rest, which are very yin in nature. The bedroom environment should therefore have a more yin bias than say the kitchen, where nourishment and productive activities (i.e. more yang) should be stimulated.

Lots of complex patterns in bedroom decor are therefore not appropriate, but this does not imply that the entire room should be completely bland and uninteresting. A little yang patterning (e.g. in a small vase) can actually emphasise the yin-ness of the rest of the design. Equally for the kitchen, it is not necessary to have wild patterns in everything – that will drive you crazy – but it is acceptable to be a little more adventurous than in the bedroom.

Other rooms in the house can be considered in a similar way (study – more yin, living room – more yang). Remember that you can 'tune' your whole home to harmonise with what you want your life to be like – more elegant and quiet or more complex and busy. As mentioned in chapter four the entrance to your home is a good place to set the 'tone' for what you want.

COLOUR

Colours and the combination of shades and intensities greatly influence our feelings and behaviours. There are five main attributes that we need to consider:

- the basic colour itself (red, green, blue etc.).

- the intensity (bright or pale).
- the shade (cherry red, maroon, neon red etc.).
- the area covered by the colour (whole wall or just a picture frame).
- the colours next to your chosen colour.

Some well established associations for specific colours are:

Red: Very yang. Strong emotions (anger and passion). Stimulates activity, excitement and sexual desires. This is a powerful colour and needs to be used with caution especially where nervous or emotionally troubled people live, or in areas intended for quiet times and rest. Too much red in a dining area can drive people to eat too quickly, causing digestive problems.

Orange: Good for revitalising, being more gentle than red, but still stimulating. Symbolises courage, confidence and creativity. Can stimulate appetite and is a good anti-depressant. Again some caution is necessary when using orange.

Yellow: Joy, happiness and creativity. Vitalising, relieves depression and anxiety. Too much yellow can cause problems for hyperactive or irritable people and needs to be balanced, if used for large areas, with calming, cooling colours.

Green: Natural cycles, transformation, growth, healing and abundance. Strong associations with the idea of peace, harmony and quietness and ideal for soothing stress or emotional problems. Too much green of one shade can be overbearing and irritating for people who need stimulation.

Turquoise: Tranquillising and relaxing. Helps in recuperation from stress or illness and calms distress or worry.

Blue: Honesty, truth, wisdom, inspiration and creativity. It is calming, with an almost sedative effect, but if over-used, can drive people into withdrawal and lethargy. Good in hot climates for inducing a cool feeling and was often used in old kitchens to keep bugs at bay.

Purple: Spirituality and dignity. Can have a balancing influence between excessive activity and relaxation and is said to decrease sensitivity to pain.

Black: Primordial darkness and negativity but also strength, stability and protection. Good in small quantities to aid introspection but is depressing when over-used.

White: Life and death, wholeness and purity. Is very good for ceilings, making them appear higher and casting an even light over a room. Also used to induce cleanliness and coolness. Appropriate for kitchens and bathrooms.

Pink: Feelings of warmth, sensitivity and love. Can be healing (if soft) but is not recommended for very temperamental people. Often recommended for bedrooms when more romance is sought.

Brown: A very 'grounding' colour for people whose attention is too scattered or too volatile. Can be restrictive and constraining in excess.

Combinations of these colours produce an infinite variety of shades and hues. Generally, brighter and stronger colours are more yang, and should be used in areas where more activity is needed. Duller or weaker shades are more yin, and are more appropriate where quiet relaxation in intended.

Within these variations, the basic colours themselves have relative yang and yin qualities, as shown in chapter two, with the red end of the spectrum being yang, yellow/green being neutral and violet extreme yin. When selecting a colour scheme for your home, or for just one part of it, you need to think about the overall image you want to create, the functions of individual areas, the characteristics of the people who use them and the overall balance of yin and yang qualities.

Brighter and stronger colours are more yang, and should be used in areas where more activity is needed

LIGHT

Moderating all choices of pattern, colour and shade is the amount and quality of light in our home. This factor also affects health, safety and personal energy levels, and must be taken into consideration when harmonising the whole environment.

Light is perceived unconsciously, but its impact is stronger than most of us realise. Lack of light (daylight especially) results in decreased mental and physical activity, increased food consumption and body weight, drowsiness and tiredness. Natural biological rhythms are also disturbed when we are not exposed to enough natural light, which in turn affects the immune system. Women are more vulnerable than men in this respect. Women also tend to be more sensitive to the colour or tint of the light and overall light distribution, while men tend to be more concerned about contrasts and luminosity of light on specific areas.

As natural daylight is most beneficial to us, we should make as much use of it as possible. Evaluate your home for the amount of daylight that comes in, and if you feel that there is not enough natural light to make you feel happy and energised, consider which of the following possibilities can help to improve the situation.

- Ensure curtains do not block any part of the window during the day.
- Clean the windows.
- Remove items on window-sills that block light.
- Move any furniture that stops light coming into the room.
- Install larger windows or additional windows.
- Replace solid panels in doors with glass panels.
- If possible clear away anything outside the windows that stops daylight or sunlight entering. Overgrown bushes and trees are typical light blockers but a porch or trellis can have a similar effect.
- Dark-coloured walls or fences close to windows could be

painted white to reflect more light into your home.

- Rooms which still do not get much natural light, should have a very light colour scheme.

As natural daylight is most beneficial to us, we should make as much use of it as possible

If there is so much daylight that your home overheats or is too bright for comfort, the obvious solution is to employ blinds or curtains or perhaps an external canopy that shields some of the direct sunlight. If further brightness reduction is necessary consider darkening the colour of walls, furniture or carpets. Sometimes shiny surfaces such as glass-topped tables and mirrors can increase glare and should therefore be moved away from direct sunlight.

For homes with insufficient daylight due to their location, or design, the extensive use of artificial light – even during the day – is recommended. Living in a gloomy environment can drain your energy and a small percentage increase in your electricity bill is worth the added vitality you get from having more light around you.

Of course every home needs additional artificial light in the hours of twilight and darkness. There are many types of lighting to choose from but some are healthier than others and some are better in certain applications than others. There are three main factors to consider when harmonising the artificial lighting in your home; these are: spectral quality, intensity and dispersion.

SPECTRAL QUALITY

Spectral quality deals with the colour or tone of the light. Our eyes have evolved to respond in specific ways to different parts of the visible spectrum. In normal healthy eyes, peak response is in the yellow/green component of daylight, with another smaller peak in the red/orange component. In other words,

If an artificial light is too dissimilar to daylight, then we are likely to feel tired when exposed to it for long periods

yellow/green and orange/red things appear to stand out more (this is why these colours are used on emergency service vehicles and clothing). Response falls to zero at and beyond the ultraviolet and infrared components of daylight. Artificial light does not contain exactly the same spectral distribution as daylight, so our eyes do not respond to it in the same way. If an artificial light is too dissimilar to daylight, then we are likely to feel tired when exposed to it for long periods.

Our skin is also a major light-absorbing organ, and requires a certain amount of light, even in the ultraviolet range, to stay healthy and keep up the production of vitamin D, or to control the hormones that keep us from feeling depressed. If you find that you tend to become depressed, lethargic and overweight in the winter months, it is worth considering the possibility that you are suffering from a lack of natural light. In this case, you can buy a 'light box' which contains a bank of special fluorescent tubes. These emit light that closely matches that of sunlight, and facing a light box for a few hours a day can relieve many of the symptoms associated with a lack of sunlight. (@)

Light from normal incandescent lamps lacks energy at the blue and ultraviolet end of the spectrum. Their warm tones can feel very comforting and restful, but they do not provide the level of ultraviolet light that we need to stay healthy. Therefore it is not good to live and work under these lights all day, especially in winter when we may also lack access to natural daylight.

Standard fluorescent lamps and tubes have a light-emission spectrum which varies considerably from natural daylight, and this is why they seem to distort colours and generally feel tiring to the eyes. They also flicker at fifty or sixty cycles per second (depending on which country you live in), which is also irritating to our eyes. I do not recommend this type of lighting for home or work places, even though they are cheaper to run than incandescent lamps.

There are now new kinds of fluorescent tubes on the market that produce much more natural light (up to ninety-six per cent compliance with daylight) and which flicker at much higher frequencies, making the effect less noticeable. These can be used in work areas and at home because they give plenty of good light for modest running costs. They may also be useful in homes where the entrance is very dark, such as in some basement flats. You may however find the light a little too harsh for rest and relaxation areas.

Energy savings can be achieved with compact fluorescent light bulbs. These are best used in areas where lights need to be on for long periods – say at least four hours at a time. The quality of light is again quite harsh compared with incandescent lamps, so they would be more appropriate for the hallway, landing or kitchen. They are also good for lamps kept on outside the house, perhaps to brighten a front entrance or to energise a 'missing' space from your house or flat, as described in chapter five.

Miniature halogen lamps provide a fairly good quality of light in terms of spectral range. They are however very intense and create strong contrasts with the light levels around them, and this can be quite stressful. They are good for highlighting shop-window displays or for reading lamps, but I would not tend to use them in general lighting configurations.

INTENSITY

The intensity of artificial light is as important as that of daylight when it comes to creating an energising environment which is safe and comfortable for daily home-based activities. Too low an intensity of light can make a home, and yourself, seem drab and can also contribute to accidents if people cannot see clearly what is around them. This is another area where it is worth comparing your home lighting with that of other people's homes or workplaces, so that you have a better idea of what feels more comfortable for you.

Psychologists have found that some gentle variation in the illumination of a space is most pleasing to humans, and this corresponds to feng shui principles. Ideally there should be a medium level of light for safe movement and comfort over most of the space. Some shadowy areas create contrast and interest to reduce visual boredom, while extra illumination should be focused on reading, writing, cooking and other kinds of detailed close work.

Since rooms are often used for multiple purposes, it is advisable to provide flexibility in the intensity of available light. For example, fix dimmer switches to the main lights in a room and have several smaller lamps and spotlights around the room for added intensity in specific areas when needed. Ordinary dimmer switches emit strong electromagnetic fields however, so I would recommend looking for specially shielded dimmers. (@)

One last point about light intensity. After the age of about forty, most people's eyes begin to loose some sensitivity, therefore, older people may need more light in order to feel safe and comfortable.

DISPERSION

Light fittings, lamp types and lamp shades control the dispersion of light. Generally, light dispersion can be considered as either direct (light reflected downwards into the room or onto a specific location), semi-direct (light is partly directed and partly reflected from ceilings or walls), indirect (most light is reflected off ceilings and walls), or diffuse (light is evenly dispersed in all directions).

For normal background lighting, semi-direct or indirect diffusion methods tend to be more comfortable. This is because very bright light sources in your field of view can, when set against a much darker background, cause great eye strain. (The light from very compact yet intense halogen lamps can be stressful in this way.) Indirect lighting can also provide the subtle variations of intensity that make it easier for our brains to judge shape and distance. Examples of semi-direct lamp fittings include translucent lamp covers, chandeliers with many crystals concealing the bulbs, and 'Chinese lantern' shades. Most indirect lamps are referred to as up-lighters, which are sold in many different styles.

Down lighting for general illumination can create a strong contrast between the ceiling and the rest of the room, and this is quite stressful. Such an effect comes from solid, opaque lamp shades and from spot lights recessed into ceilings.

Provided that the light does not shine directly into your field of view, strong down lighting is best suited to illuminating small work areas or specific objects such as a painting hanging on a wall. In this way your attention is drawn to the key images and symbols in your home. The effect of these images and symbols is, however, the subject of the next chapter.

CHAPTER SEVEN

Images and symbols

Whenever we sense something either through vision, taste, touch or smell, our minds actually call up a great amount of other information about the object, in addition to what our senses are telling us. So, if your eyes happen to glance upon the china dog that Auntie Flo brought you from her trip to the seaside years ago, at some level your mind brings up and very quickly processes all kinds of data associated with Auntie Flo, dogs, seasides, etc. Some of this data may generate good feelings – for example the fun times that you had with Auntie Flo – while other associations may generate less positive feelings, if for example you were attacked by a dog when you were young.

Almost everything in our environment conjures up complex feelings of one kind or another, so it is advisable to understand what the most important of these things are, what effects they are having, and how we can change them to create a more harmonious space.

In this chapter we will concentrate on the most common items that we put in our homes and which are intended to be looked at and appreciated. Such items include photographs of family and friends, pictures of places we have visited, posters, paintings, models, statues, icons, plants and flowers.

PHOTOGRAPHS

It can be beneficial to have photos of friends and family around the home but only under certain conditions.

The photographs should be of people with whom you have far more positive associations than negative ones. We all have disagreements and conflicts with those we love (sometimes especially with those we love), but if the overall experience of being involved with this person is very positive, then it is acceptable to keep their image in your space. If the person reminds you of unhappy situations, exploitation, abandonment, deceit, mistrust, betrayal, etc., then remove their image from your environment, or at least from any space where your eyes may inadvertently fall upon it.

Do not have too many photos from the past – a few photos may be acceptable, but covering your walls with them indicates a paranoia and unwillingness to let go of what was, and to live in the present. I have frequently seen homes where large areas of wall space are devoted to photos of parents, lost husbands or wives, or old school days. A preponderance of such images can subconsciously stop you from dealing with current situations and block you from feeling in harmony with the present.

One of the principles in feng shui suggests that the most appropriate place for photos of parents or people from the past is around the centre of the wall on the left side of your home or a room, as seen when you enter it. The opposite wall (on the right as you enter the home or room) is associated with the future and is a good place for photos of children.

PICTURES

Pictures of places, whether photos, posters or paintings, can also have an impact on emotional comfort and feelings of harmony in the home. The most important factors are subject matter, colouring and style.

Almost everything in our environment conjures up complex feelings of one kind or another

Scenes of isolation and desolation in your environment can quickly become representative of the quality of life you experience. One of my clients complained that no matter what he did, nothing much ever seemed to happen in his life. It was no surprise to find pictures of desolate sand dunes, long, empty beaches and barren snowscapes (and all in dull, faded colours) scattered around his house and office. We suggested replacing these pictures with scenes of active and energetic groups of people as one might see in a busy market place, a dance hall or café. Similarly, another client who had been looking for a partner for several years, had pictures of single or lonely looking women in every room of her flat – including the bathroom. We replaced these with pictures of happy couples to create the 'energy' of relationship in her life.

Homes where arguments and stress are prevalent are often adorned with pictures of danger, death and destruction as associated with hunting scenes, dead fish, wars and battles, weapons, fighter planes and bombers, stormy seas, and so on. A harmonious home is no place for such images. Instead, introduce beautiful pictures of healthy landscapes, people working or playing in harmony, or other inspiring images.

Some people tend to choose pictures which have rather dull, unexciting colours or just black and white images. This can also lead to a rather dull and unexciting environment if not balanced with some brighter pictures. I am not suggesting that every picture in the home should be grossly flamboyant and loud, but it is important to be aware of the general tone of the pictures we have around us and the corresponding flavour of our lives.

Do not have too many photos from the past

The style of pictures also has subtle influences on our subconscious feelings. Abstract pictures, dark images and lots of points and sharp angles can represent confusion and aggression, and are not conducive to harmony. One client was very proud of a painting of New York that was given to her by a friend. This was indeed a great work of art, but the picture was semi-abstract, mainly in deep blues, greys and black and depicted the buildings, piers and seascape with an array of dagger-like strokes. It was hung outside a bedroom and was painted by someone who died in unpleasant circumstances. Needless to say, the client constantly felt overwhelmed and exhausted. It is worth making a general point here about the difference between art and home decor. What you have in your home is to some degree an extension of yourself or your self image, and strongly colours your experience of life. Therefore be very careful about the images around you and what they mean. If a great work of art has negative connotations it is better displayed in a dedicated art gallery rather than a home.

Abstract pictures, dark images and lots of points and sharp angles can represent confusion and aggression

OBJECTS

The potential effects of other art or symbolic objects around the home are similar to those of pictures. Items that are not conducive to a harmonious atmosphere and which I have seen displayed on walls or furniture in clients' homes include guns, swords, warrior masks, spears and shields, model war planes and missiles. On the other hand, fresh flowers, symbols of love such as pairs of birds, dolphins or people, elegant vases, candlesticks, statues of positive religious and mythical figures or other sculptures in soft colours and curved shapes, can all contribute to an image of harmony. However, too many such objects – even harmonious ones – can create a sense of confusion and clutter, which has the opposite effect.

Many books on feng shui refer to fish tanks containing several goldfish as being a great symbol of wealth, prosperity, movement and energy. This can be true, but understand that the total image must actually represent this movement and freedom. I once had a client who, after reading a popular book on feng shui, proudly showed me her fish tank placed in the wealth corner of her flat. She had bought the right number of fish according to the book, but had placed them in such a small tank that they could hardly move. The actual image created in this case was more like torture and living death than energy and freedom. She was concerned that her efforts at feng shui had not created the desired result!

There is a huge variety of other images and symbols we can use to create a specific atmosphere or tone in a home, or to stimulate the creation of a particular life experience. The numbers of such items in your home is also of significance. Again, use your imagination or refer to additional texts on these matters. (@)

PLANTS AND FLOWERS

Spiky-leaved plants can be a useful stimulant

The shapes of plants and flowers in our homes and gardens can conjure up a surprising array of subliminal messages. For example, that big cactus with long pointed spines and vicious spikes in the hall says to anyone entering the home 'danger, keep out, go away'. If your friends (if you have any left that is) don't come around any more, or if you get a strange sense of trepidation at the thought of going home, it may well have something to do with your taste in house plants. Spiky-leaved plants can be a useful stimulant in an environment that is a bit too quiet or lethargic, but be conscious of the potential for fights with your spouse or partner if cacti or other plants with pointed leaves dominate the bedroom, lounge or kitchen areas. I suggest you check the effect of throwing out the spiky plants before throwing out your spouse or partner!

To smooth tensions and soften the atmosphere at home, choose plants that have round leaves (jade plant for example) or elegant flowing foliage like the Boston Fern.

ARRANGEMENT

Think also of the arrangement of items in your home. We generally think of positive or progressive movement as being from left to right and from lower to higher as we look at them. If possible therefore, arrange your sculptures so that they look to the right or place them in a sequence with the shortest item on the left of the display, and the tallest on the right. This idea also applies to pictures. First, select images which tend to face or lean towards the right, and where any slopes run from the lower left to upper right. One client was in a situation where many aspects of his life seemed to be on the decline. Interestingly, the large painting opposite his bed was of a cyclist speeding downhill towards the bottom left of the picture. Another client who was struggling to keep a new business going had many downward looking images in his living room including an ivy plant dangling down from a high shelf, low-hanging lamp shades and a sequence of pictures on the wall which were hung in a downward slope from left to right. These details may seem at first glance to be insignificant, but they all actually contribute, little by little and cumulatively over time, to feelings of negativity and despair, or at least to a sense of struggle and effort.

Many other images and symbols are brought into our homes through electronic devices such as televisions, radios, computers and so on. But these also create another 'atmosphere' which is not obvious to our primary senses. This effect is the electromagnetic environment, the impact of which is discussed in the next chapter.

CHAPTER EIGHT

Electromagnetic stress

We have all evolved in an electromagnetic field – the natural one created by the earth itself. This magnetic field is generally fairly stable although variations in intensity do occur over distance and time as the result of interactions with cosmic radiation from the sun and the magnetic fields of the sun and other planets. Analysis of volcanic rock from the deep ocean floor suggests that every 29,000 years or so, there has been a reversal of the magnetic poles of the earth. How this affects life on the planet we do not know – yet.

Other, very localised natural disturbances to the earth's magnetic field have also been observed for hundreds, if not thousands of years. Some are referred to as ley lines in the UK, and where different ley lines cross is frequently the site of an ancient monument or the altar of an ancient church or cathedral. Note that such 'energised' sites were used for special purposes – not for living on. Other forms of magnetic field disturbances seem to cause a lowering of the human energy field, lethargy, depression and even serious illnesses such as cancer. This phenomenon is called 'geopathic stress', and appears to be related to geologic faults in the earth's crust, fast flowing underground streams of trapped water, major underground earth works such as foundations for high-rise buildings, main sewers and railways. It is worth mentioning that full scientific investigations of these phenomena still need to be conducted, but the effects are well known and have been detected by dowsers for hundreds of years. (@)

By and large however, human beings have evolved over the last million-or-so years to exist happily in the earth's natural electromagnetic environment, avoiding places where the natural energy did not feel right.

ELECTROMAGNETIC FIELDS IN THE HOME

You may wonder what the earth's electromagnetic field has to do with harmonising your home. The relevance is that the electromagnetic environment of the modern urban home is quite different from that of our ancestors. We are, for example, constantly bombarded from the outside with microwave radiation from television, radar and telecommunications transmitters both on the ground and in space. Also, many people live close to the strong electromagnetic fields surrounding power distribution cables, mains transformers and electric railways. Inside our homes we generate unnatural electric fields from the motors in washing machines, vacuum cleaners, fans, electric cookers, microwave ovens and various other household devices, and from the screens of television sets and computers. Even the electrical cables running round the house generate a small, but detectable electric field.

Experience to date indicates that, on average, the human body tolerates these strong electromagnetic fields quite well for short periods, although it is difficult to know if our personal energy levels and overall health would be better without them. It is also important to recognise that some people (often women more than men) are far more sensitive to these fields than others. You have probably read of children who slept close

Reduce exposure to unnatural electromagnetic fields

to large electrical transformers dying of brain tumours, or of people living under overhead power transmission cables experiencing various nervous system disorders. Ultimately it is the combination of stresses (electromagnetic fields, air and water pollution, unhealthy personal habits, low quality food, chemicals in household products, persistent and excessive noise, overwork, emotional problems, lack of exercise, cluttered and chaotic environments, inappropriate interior design and decor, etc.) on our minds and bodies that trigger persistent or serious illness and distress. It seems to me therefore that we should endeavour to eliminate as many of these as possible, since we may never know which one will be the 'straw that breaks the camel's back'.

To reduce exposure to unnatural electromagnetic fields in the home, here are a few simple suggestions:

- Only have televisions, radios, hi-fi and computers switched on when there is good reason. Recognise when these devices are used just out of habit rather than to meet a genuine need.
- If you are watching a small television set or using a computer, sit at least one metre away from the screen. Sit at least two metres from a large television screen.
- Never place a television or computer screen close to where someone sleeps, whether in the same room or an adjacent one – electromagnetic fields pass through walls as if they do not exist. If you live in a semi-detached house, terrace house or flat, you may need to check with your neighbours that your respective televisions are away from adjoining bedroom walls.
- Avoid having any electrical devices near the bed, and never go to bed with an electric blanket switched on or even connected to the power supply.
- Use hand tools and household gadgets in preference to electrically driven ones where possible.
- Put plenty of evergreen plants and ferns close to electrical

equipment, especially computer and television screens. These are supposed to reduce the de-ionising effect of strong electromagnetic fields. The Torch Cactus is also very good in this respect.** (@)

- Put a conductive acrylic filter over your computer screen to reduce the electromagnetic field. It is most important that the filter is an exact fit otherwise you may create a secondary field that is worse than the original one. As far as I know, such filters are not available for televisions. **
- Place the television and computer monitors on cork tiles (rough side up). Cork has been found to suppress electromagnetic fields. **
- Avoid sleeping on beds with metal frames, steel-sprung mattresses and electric blankets, and avoid sitting for long periods on metal-framed or metal-sprung chairs. Wooden furniture is best, with natural fibre-filled mattresses or upholstery. (@)

(** This information comes from the Dulwich Health Society in London.)

More expensive methods of reducing the tiny electric fields from household wiring include the installation of demand switches on the mains fuse or circuit breaker box to isolate circuits which are not in use (@), rewiring the home (or just the bedroom perhaps) with electrically shielded cables.

You may have seen advertisements for passive devices that promise to 'neutralise' negative electrical fields from the home and create a 'positive energy field'. The manufacturers of some of these devices claim to have based their design on various electromagnetic theorems. Unfortunately I have not been able to gather sufficient unbiased information so far to determine the validity of these claims or to test their effectiveness outside the laboratory environment. Another common factor is that they all seem quite expensive – some costing hundreds of pounds. (@)

Other devices, rather than suppressing or masking the electromagnetic fields, claim instead to reduce their effect on an individual when carried close to the body. These claims also need careful investigation. (@)

GEOPATHIC STRESS

Probably the most dangerous, yet least acknowledged form of electromagnetic contamination is geopathic stress. For most of human history, people have lived very close to nature and were probably more aware of sites that had strange magnetic forces around them (even though they had no idea of what it was that caused these feelings), and chose to live or sleep elsewhere. The homes and businesses of modern urban society are situated for economic convenience rather than for environmental health, and our hurried, stress-driven life styles leave no space for developing or experiencing the more subtle sensations and information that our bodies can give us. As a result, many people are working and sleeping on geopathic stress zones which can be a major contributor to all kinds of mental and physical illness.

So how would you know if your bedroom were situated on a geopathic stress line? Here are a number of questions that can help you to determine whether your room is affected.

- Even if you look after plants correctly, do they still wither in this room?
- Do you consistently suffer from poor sleep when in this room?
- Do you keep getting strange illnesses that are reluctant to clear up?
- Do you often feel tired and exhausted, even first thing in the morning?
- Do you suffer from unexplained aches and pains?
- Did the people who previously slept in this room have poor health?

- Do cats like to be in this room?
- If babies or young children use this room, do you persistently find them in the morning squeezed into a corner or one end of the cot or bed?

How would you know if your bedroom were situated on a geopathic stress line?

If the answer to more than four or five of these questions is 'yes', it is worth checking the house for geopathic stress. This is done by dowsing which you can learn for yourself from books or courses, or you can hire an experienced person to do it for you. (@)

If you suspect that geopathic stress is present in your home the most important step is to move beds or any chairs where you sit for long periods each day, as far away as possible from the suspected geopathic stress line. Some people may even move to a different bedroom to escape it. In addition there are a number of devices on the market that can be plugged into the electrical ring main circuit and claim to reduce or eliminate geopathic stress. My experience with these devices has been mixed. Sometimes they seem to work, while in other situations they appear to have little or no effect. I think that we still do not understand the physics of this phenomenon enough to produce entirely reliable cures. Some people suggest placing mineral crystals such as salt, quartz or amethyst on or near the geopathic stress lines. It seems that the different minerals affect specific levels or types of geopathic stress, making it necessary to dowse for the cure as well as the presence of the phenomenon. Another common solution is to drive metal rods or tubes into the soil along the geopathic stress lines. To determine the type of metal, length and thickness of the rods or tubes to be used in any particular situation, expert dowsers often use a pendulum method of dowsing, but that goes beyond the scope of this book.

Whereas the ways of dealing with geopathic stress described

above seem to require 'custom' designed solutions for each individual case, we have recently discovered a new approach which seems to offer a universal solution i.e. it can neutralise a wide range of geopathic stress forms. It is currently being tested. (@)

It would be very difficult to make any home feel harmonious if the inhabitants are sleeping, or attempting to sleep, on geopathic stress. If you, or a member of your family are experiencing inexplicable emotional, mental or physical health problems at home, it is worth while checking for geopathic stress and calling in an expert to devise a solution with you. It could save your life!

If you have eliminated electromagnetic stress as much as possible, and still feel ill, you may like to check some of the products in your home for toxicity; and this is covered in the next chapter.

CHAPTER NINE

Toxic threats to harmony

A harmonious home is a healthy home – its constituents support you rather than hurt you. Underneath all of the magic and mysticism surrounding many descriptions of feng shui, lie the original guidelines for establishing healthy, safe and secure places to live. In general the homes of today are infinitely more supportive than those of past ages, but we have also introduced many materials that can have very damaging effects on our biological systems. It is important to know what they are, where they come from, and what to do about them. This chapter identifies some of the main sources of toxic chemicals in modern homes and suggests alternatives or practical counter measures.

Few of us (although the number is growing rapidly) experience severe immediate reactions to normal household materials and products when used occasionally. We therefore tend to treat them as benign or fairly harmless. Unfortunately, it is becoming clear that a large number of common items in the home have almost imperceptible, yet cumulative effects, and when lots of them are present in the home together over long periods of time, along with stressful life styles and less than healthy eating habits, our immune systems start to fail and we create conditions in which serious illness can develop. This is neither harmonious nor fun! Obviously, toxic chemicals can cause a lot of damage if we ingest them directly or if they come into contact with sensitive parts of the body, such as the eyes. However, toxic chemicals are also absorbed through the skin and when we breathe in their fumes.

Physical reactions to contaminants include skin rashes, sore eyes, nausea, headaches and asthma-type symptoms. Secondary reactions may show up as fits of depression, fatigue and confusion. There is also evidence that the immune system of children is under so much stress from unnatural contaminants that it never has a chance to develop properly resulting in the dramatic rise in allergy based illnesses and other disorders which were very rare in the West before the early 1900s, and which are still rare in remote rural communities elsewhere in the world.

HOUSEHOLD CLEANERS

These are some of the most dangerous items in any home, with components that can produce effects ranging from sore eyes to terminal cancer, and the average household may use up to twenty kilograms of them per year. There is a large range of poisons in these products and so I offer below simpler and safer alternatives for common cleansing tasks. (@)

- White vinegar and water in a ratio of about one to three, makes an excellent window-cleaning fluid, and can also be used for a general wipe-down.
- A paste made from baking soda and water makes a cleaner for delicate surfaces (add water to soda and blend until the right consistency is reached).
- Baking soda, salt and water

Simpler and safer alternatives for common cleansing tasks

makes a more abrasive mixture for scrubbing. (Make up quantities according to your immediate need, adding more salt if extra abrasion is needed.)

- Borax (1 tsp), washing soda (1 tsp), white vinegar (2 tblsp) and 2 cups of hot water is good for really tough cleaning jobs.
- Borax (1 tsp), white vinegar (3 tblsp) and 2 cups of hot water makes a good bathroom cleaner.
- There are also various commercially produced non-toxic household cleaning products. (@)

TOILETRIES

Less obvious contributors to stress exist in those products that we tend to keep in the bathroom. Many popular skin- and hair-care products contain an array of petroleum-based compounds that can aggravate our immune system, hormonal balance, and general energy levels.

Common brands of toothpaste for example, contain an array of oil-based chemicals, artificial flavours and colourings. There are alternative brands however that use vegetable-derived products and are therefore safer. Basic toothpaste is made from ordinary bicarbonate of soda, so it is quite easy to make your own – you just have to get used to a different taste and texture. (@)

Many skin- and hair-care products contain materials that actually cause long-term damage by blocking the normal functioning of skin pores and hair structures. So if you wish to stay genuinely healthy, young and beautiful, avoid soaps, shampoos and lotions that contain:

- Mineral oils: Derived from petroleum, these sit on the surface of the skin, giving the impression of moisturising, but in fact clogging the pores and potentially leading to acne and cancer.
- Formaldehyde: Used as a disinfectant and preservative, but causes severe irritation to mucus membranes and skin and is

a known carcinogen.

- Paraffin: Oily and relatively harmless to the skin when very pure, but the commercial versions often contain irritating contaminants.
- Lanolin: Made from sheep glands and can cause rashes on sensitive skin.
- Petroleum jelly: Very greasy, and once on the skin is hard to remove completely. As a result, dirt and other toxins from the atmosphere get stuck to the skin surface and congregate in skin pores causing irritation and spots.
- Borax: Sodium Borate is a harsh tanning agent used in the leather industry, and is a powerful component of oven cleaners. It is also used as a preservative and texturiser in many face and body creams!
- Proplyene Glycol and Sodium Laurel Sulphate: Easily pass into the blood system and get stuck in the liver where secondary problems originate (e.g. vision loss).

There are several brands of safer cosmetic and body-care products available in some shops or by mail order. (@)

ORGANIC SOLVENTS AND OTHER CHEMICALS

You have probably heard of young people who either died or caused considerable damage to their brains through solvent abuse. These same solvents, (formaldehyde, xylene, toluene, benzene) and up to three hundred other nerve-damaging and carcinogenic agents, make up and evaporate from hundreds of common brands of consumer products including toiletries and cosmetics, perfumes, permanent-press fabrics, paints, cleaning solvents, paper towels, grocery bags, wall coverings and carpets. Organic

Avoid bringing toxins into the home

solvents are also emitted from adhesives including the glue used in chipboard and plywood. This means that a great deal of modern furniture is a source of toxic gas. It may take many months for the solvents in paint to evaporate (they are there even if you can't smell them), and it may take years for the toxic vapours in chipboard furniture, carpeting and plastics to become insignificant.

These chemicals can instigate, aggravate or contribute to allergies, asthma, fatigue, headaches, respiratory problems and nervous-system disorders. If any of these symptoms upset the harmony between you and your home, then it needs to be resolved using one of the methods described below.

The best solution is to avoid bringing toxins into the home in the first place by using alternatives to chipboard and toxic paints, avoiding plastics, vinyl-coated materials and polyurethane foam, man-made carpeting materials and other fabrics, etc. Several brands of non-toxic paints and wood treatments are now available, and there is a wide range of natural fabrics, pure cotton bed linen, floor coverings, carpets and backing materials. However, toxins are so pervasive in the common products that we buy, it is almost impossible to avoid them totally. But we can start to improve the situation by making more informed choices about certain items – perhaps selecting borax and vinegar next time you clean up the kitchen, or buying a non-toxic paint when you redecorate the bedroom. As more and more people go for domestic products that are in harmony with our physical and biological nature, manufacturers and retailers will find it increasingly cost effective to provide them instead of products that can harm us – and the environment generally. (@)

Ensure that there is plenty of ventilation through the house

If you feel that you may already be affected by the materials and products in your home, it is best to ensure that there is plenty of ventilation through the house to allow a complete change of air every hour or so. In this way toxic fumes are less likely to build up to dangerous levels. This is especially important for the bedroom at night.

Another option is to keep plenty of plants in the home. Many well known house plants actually absorb some of the toxic chemicals, either through their roots or leaves. This process is aided and abetted by the microbes that live in the soil in the plant pot. Here is a list of examples taken from Eco Friendly House Plants by B. C. Wolverton (@). The plants selected are aesthetically pleasing from a feng shui point of view and are also effective and easy to maintain:

Boston fern, areca palm, bamboo palm, rubber plant, English ivy, ficus, peace lily, dumb cane, schefflera, king of hearts, dwarf banana, lily turf, spider plant, dwarf azalea and tulip.

COMBUSTION GASES

The by-products of burning gas, coal or oil include a range of poisonous gases such as carbon monoxide, carbon dioxide, sulphur and nitrous oxides. Thus any combustion process that occurs inside the home and which does not have an exhaust system connected directly to the outside (e.g. gas cookers, self-standing oil-fired heaters) are serious sources of toxins. When these devices are used therefore, plenty of ventilation is essential.

INSECTICIDES

The products we bring into the home to kill insects like flies, moths and ants, also act on our biological system. Safer ways to deal with insect pests are:

- ***Flies***: Grow basil and mint plants by the door or windows in the main rooms affected by flies. Also put orange or lemon peel or cloves around the windows. Flies apparently dislike the smell of these plants and fruits, and will therefore tend to keep away.

- ***Moths***: Lavender or cedar wood shavings in wardrobes and drawers will keep moths away from your clothes.
- ***Ants***: If you can find where they are entering the home, sprinkle chilli powder or dried mint in the area. Growing mint plants outside will also help keep ants at bay.

ALUMINIUM

Aluminium is believed to be a key contributor to Alzheimer's disease. In fact the disease itself was first identified about twenty years after aluminium came into common use. (@) You can reduce exposure to aluminium by:

- Using iron, steel, enamelled, or glass cooking pots and utensils instead of aluminium ones.
- Avoid baking powders and cake mixes that contain aluminium compounds.
- Avoid antacid medicines that use aluminium compounds.
- Processed cheese may also contain excessive amounts of aluminium.
- Avoid roll-on, spray and stick deodorants that contain aluminium.

CHAPTER TEN

A breath of fresh air

The most penetrating aspect of our home environment, and yet what we are often least conscious of, is the air we breathe, the literal atmosphere of the home.

A harmonious atmosphere smells clean and fresh. It does not hold heavy stale odours or feel 'stuffy'. Breathing is essential for life and as philosophies and religions have asserted for thousands of years, the quality of life is affected by the quality of breathing – how we breathe and what we breathe. Slow deep breaths are conducive to calmness and relaxation and the effective use of energy. Breathing fresh air implies taking in fresh ideas, perceptions and insights. Breathing stale air implies taking in the same old problems, worries and attitudes.

Beathing stale air implies taking in the same old problems, worries and attitudes

The most common causes of stale air are dampness in timber or plaster, decaying food particles, and volatile grease and fat deposits.

DEALING WITH DAMP

There are well established technologies and companies capable of resolving most damp problems. It is worth making the investment and solving these problems as not only will your home smell better, but there will be less humidity and mould or fungus spores, which can cause health problems, and the structural standard (and hence value) of your home will be maintained. Dampness is usually due to leaking water pipes and drains or a damaged damp-proofing system in the structural walls of the building. Condensation can also cause damp conditions if prolonged. Condensation is caused by moisture in the relatively warm air from baths, showers, cooking and gas or oil heaters, hitting much colder walls.

In order to prevent condensation:

- Avoid free-standing oil or gas burners, which produce water vapour as a by-product of combustion.
- Increase ventilation rates (use extractor fans or open windows).
- Increase room temperature so that the walls get warmer (this is probably not energy efficient in most areas).

FOOD AND COOKING SMELLS

Smells from food particles and grease deposits are the most pernicious and hide in all kinds of inaccessible places. These particles come from fats and oils evaporated into the air from frying pans, and from cigarette or pipe fumes. They condense over every conceivable surface, giving off odours for months. The main solutions to this kind of problem are:

- Find ways of preparing and serving food so that particles are less likely to fall behind cupboards, cookers, fridges or other hard-to-clean areas.
- Look at the possibility of modifying your diet by reducing the consumption of fat (this can also have other health benefits) and change cooking methods to reduce the amount of open-pan frying.
- Do not smoke indoors.
- Have a really good clean up of the kitchen area, including the walls, floor, ceiling and any fabrics (e.g. curtains) to remove any food remnants or traces of condensed oil, fat or nicotine.
- Keep an extractor fan running and/or open a window while cooking foods that could contaminate your kitchen. An alternative to an electric fan is a simple plastic ventilator containing a fan that operates when there is a difference of

pressure caused by natural air currents, between the inside and outside air.

VENTILATION

A continuous exchange of air while we are inside the home is important, not only to purge cooking smells and other odours, but to clear out toxic fumes from chemicals and heaters of various kinds as described in chapter nine, and from the chemicals we (and our pets) as biological systems, release into the air.

There are standard recommended airflows through buildings based on the number of people in them and the volume of space. However for most people at home such measurements are impractical. The best method is to experiment with different ventilation options, depending on outside air temperature, wind speed and direction and the amount and type of indoor activity. Generally, some airflow through the home and through individual rooms is necessary to inhibit air stagnation.

If you live in a densely populated urban area, the air from outside may not be very pure, or at the right temperature or humidity for comfort. For temperate and cooler climates, fresh air may need to be warmed – thermal harmony is as important as any other form. Central heating systems tend to be more efficient at this than other types of heating and if oil or gas fired, tend to create fewer noxious gases inside the home than open fires. It is important to feel warm and comfortable: it is hard to relax if you are cold. Remember too that you can create a sense of warmth by decorating the rooms in warm colours.

It is especially important that the air in bedrooms is kept fresh while we are asleep

It is especially important that the air in bedrooms is kept fresh while we are asleep because we are less capable of eliminating toxins when in a very relaxed state. 'Fresh' however does not mean freezing cold – which is the typical British assumption. Very cold air can make you vulnerable to respiratory infections when the metabolic rate slows down at night. Therefore rid the bedroom of as many toxic pollutants as possible using the information given here and in chapter nine.

For people living in hot and tropical climates, the opposite thermal problem often occurs – the outside air is too warm. Assuming that air conditioning is not used, it is still possible to 'cool off' a space by decorating in cool colours (blue, green or white) and installing images of water or miniature waterfalls or fountains.

In very humid (i.e. water-type) situations, feng shui principles suggest an environment containing lots of wood and earth elements – perhaps ceramic flooring or ceramic pots and large wooden furniture. See the section on balancing the five elements in chapter two.

Chapter nine gives details of the numerous toxic fumes that are emitted into the home environment. One partial solution to this pollution is to eliminate toxic materials and products from the home, but there are other pollutants that are more difficult to reduce – these are dust, and mould and fungus spores.

MOULD AND FUNGUS SPORES

Mould and fungus spores can contribute to sinus and bronchial problems, fatigue, depression and headaches. They most commonly appear on the grouting between bathroom tiles, on shower curtains and around the edges of baths and sinks. They are less visible, but still present, in carpets and mattresses, old books and newspapers and around the refrigerator door seal – in fact anywhere that is dank and damp.

Some solutions to this problem are:

- Keep areas where water collects well ventilated and/or warm and dry.
- Regularly clean areas where mould spores grow with borax solution.
- Dry out damp carpets or other fabrics.
- Turn and air mattresses regularly.
- Fix any leaking pipes or structural damp problems.
- Get rid of, or shut away in a dry place, any old books and papers.

DUST

Dust comes in many forms. It may be tiny particles of carbon from vehicle exhausts; cigarette smoke or fires; filaments of fabrics; skin scales from humans, pets or insects; food particles; powders or sprays. One of the greatest causes is the infamous microscopic dust-mite and its even more microscopic droppings.

I feel that I must explain more about the dust-mite, but it does not make pleasant reading – so skip this bit if you are squeamish. Dust-mites cannot be seen by the naked eye, yet they exist in their millions in mattresses, bedding, carpets, furniture and curtains. They thrive in warm humid conditions such as are found in thickly carpeted, over-heated homes. Although their life span is only about ten weeks, each female can produce up to eighty eggs in that time. The mites themselves are difficult to extract even with the most powerful vacuum cleaners, but the eggs and droppings can be collected provided that your vacuum cleaner has an extra very fine filter attached to it. If this has made you feel worried, I suggest that you make a cup of tea and sit down – because worse is to follow!

Dust consists of particles that can cause a vast array of allergic reactions as well as carry bacteria and viruses that spread colds and flu. If you frequently, and during all seasons of the year, experience a sore throat, runny nose, sneezing, strange rashes and even bouts of confusion, you may be extra sensitive to dust in the atmosphere and need to take precautions such as the following:

- If you have doors or windows facing a busy road keep them shut when traffic pollution is at its worst.
- Thoroughly and frequently clean the home to remove dust particles from flat surfaces, window-sills, bookshelves, window-frames, door-frames, table-tops and so on, as well as carpets, upholstery, etc. Do not use dry dusters or brooms. These only spread dust into the air – it then settles on the floor or in your lungs. Use damp cloths or a vacuum cleaner.
- Open windows while cleaning to vent any dust that gets into the air.
- Wash bedding weekly at high temperatures and duvets and pillows at least monthly.
- Use dust-mite proof covers for mattresses, duvets and pillows. (@)
- Replace pillows and cushions once or twice a year.
- Steam clean soft furnishings and curtains.
- Use roller blinds instead of curtains where possible.
- Minimise wall-to-wall carpeting.
- Enclose open shelves to reduce dust collecting on surfaces.
- Avoid eating while walking around the house.
- Minimise the use of free-standing oil or gas fires or open wood or coal fires.
- Do not smoke indoors.
- Use non-toxic dust-mite and allergen-control sprays on water-tolerant fabrics and carpets (but not bedding). (@)

If pollen is a problem for you, then keeping all windows closed may be necessary during periods of high pollen count. This implies that you need to take special care with the chemicals and materials you bring into your home and to keep the place as clean as possible during low pollen count periods.

IONISATION

Have you noticed when you stand on the seashore in a clean environment, how exhilarating the air feels and how our lungs almost crave to consume more of it, automatically changing from shallow to deeper breathing. What we are experiencing is the effect of negatively charged oxygen molecules, which are created naturally by sunlight, lightning and water spray.

Urban environments polluted with lots of chemicals and particulate matter and strong electromagnetic fields may contain only twenty per cent of the natural amount of negative ions. This can contribute to bronchial and sinus irritations and to feelings of lethargy and dullness.

To improve the proportion of negative oxygen ions in the home and to create a fresher atmosphere it is necessary to reduce the causes of negative ion depletion and then to apply a method for generating more negative ions.

To reduce ion depletions:

- Follow the steps described earlier for reducing dust and chemical pollutants.
- Buy carpets, rugs and fabrics made of natural materials which do not generate static electricity as man-made fibres do.
- Switch off televisions and computers when they are not really needed. The cathode ray tubes (the picture display systems) create strong magnetic fields which reduce the number of negative ions in the air around them.

To generate negative ions there are three main options. Do bear in mind that none of these can fully compensate for the drastic loss of negative ions in bad urban air, but even making some effort at improvement will instill in our minds the idea that our home is a little more natural and harmonious than it might have been before.

- Water spray: a miniature waterfall or fountain in the home may have some small effect, but any spray or vapour should be exposed to daylight or some other source of ultraviolet light.

- Plants: the metabolism of some plants is known to produce negatively charged ions. These include ferns, evergreens and the torch cactus.
- Ionisers: these electronic devices that generate negative oxygen ions come in various types and sizes but can have a number of drawbacks. Their internal and structural components may add toxic chemicals to the atmosphere and the electromagnetic fields they produce may create worse problems than those they are designed to solve.

Commercial air-fresheners in spray cans or in the form of evaporating tablets are the least effective way of creating 'fresh' air. They work in different ways but all introduce more toxic chemicals into the environment such as formaldehyde, naphthalene, xylene, ethanol and phenol. Some work by interfering with or blocking the nerve endings in your nose so that, in effect, they are deactivated. Others chemically neutralise the odour or just cover it up with a stronger smell. Healthier options include having fresh flowers in the home, distributing small bowls of baking soda or white wine vinegar around the house, vaporising natural aromatherapy oils or using herbal pot-pourri.

If using ventilation fans or opening windows is your only choice for letting fresh air into your home, you may expose yourself to another major irritant – noise.

Commercial air-fresheners in spray cans or in the form of evaporating tablets are the least effective way of creating 'fresh' air

CHAPTER ELEVEN

Sounds ominous

Although the term harmony is more often associated with sound, we rarely think of sound as a key ingredient in the overall harmony of our environment. From the perspective of auditory stimuli, the typical urban home environment is far from natural. Even many rural locations are polluted with a range of irksome, mechanical sounds from road traffic, aircraft and farm machinery.

It is important to be aware of the constant assault that noise places upon us so that we can take at least some steps to reduce the stresses that it creates. These stresses can increase blood pressure, decrease immunity, and cause neurological disorders, irritability and insomnia. If you have an existing illness, constant or erratic sound can not only disrupt recovery but can actually make matters worse. Noise affects us less if it is linked to some personal benefit. Other people's noise, such as that from telephones and mobile phones, televisions or hi-fi systems used by others in your home or neighbouring homes, can be devastating.

One of the main problems with noise is that it is so penetrating and insidious. We may be too busy, or otherwise too distracted even to identify, let alone deal with, the various noise irritants in our homes. To help you, here are some examples in addition to those mentioned above: refrigerator, washing machine, kitchen mixer, drills, saws, road works, car or motorcycle repairs, ticking/chiming clocks, computers, creaking door hinges, buzzing fluorescent lamps, extractor fans, dripping taps, lawn mowers, barking dogs, hammering and garbage collection.

People who live in or near busy roads or shopping areas may also have to endure the noise of delivery vehicles, bleeping pedestrian crossings, police and emergency service sirens, heavy traffic and so on.

NOISE FROM OUTSIDE THE HOME

You may have no control over noise that originates from beyond the boundaries of your home, but there are a number of ways of dealing with this sort of problem:

• Explain to the originators of the noise the problems they are causing and try to find a solution.

• Check with the local authority to determine if any noise abatement by-laws are being broken.

• If possible, construct a high, solid wall or double fence between your home and the noise source.

• Plant dense evergreen hedges between your home and the noise source.

• Install double-glazing, (or triple-glazing if the noise is severe) and keep windows and doors shut, at least on the side of the house where the noise comes from.

• Ear plugs may help.

• Heavy curtains completely covering the windows on the noisy side of the home can absorb some sound.

• Symbolically, suggest to your subconscious that the irritation caused by the noise is being reflected back and dispersed from your home, by placing a small convex mirror or other shiny convex object so that it faces the source of the noise (e.g. on or over the front door, in a window).

• Keep cassette tapes or CDs of soothing, quiet music or other natural sounds. Play them to yourself through headphones when external noise strikes.

NOISE FROM INSIDE THE HOME

Although you may have more control over noise that is created within your own home, the problem can be just as stressful. Here are some potential solutions:

- Make a 'peace treaty' with those people in your home who tend to create a lot of noise. For example, suggest that they use headphones with the hi-fi, radio or television or maintain certain times or certain days as 'quiet'. It may also be appropriate to suggest that certain noisy activities be banned from the house, especially if they are not supporting or contributing to your life.
- Fix any little irritating noises such as creaking doors, dripping taps, rattling windows.
- Turn off extractor fans as soon as they are no longer needed.
- Use washing machines and dishwashers less often and more efficiently, i.e. only with a full load.
- Use hand, rather than electrical, tools in the workshop, kitchen or around the house where feasible.
- Mow the lawn less often.
- Turn off televisions, radios, etc. unless there is something interesting or restful and pleasant to listen to.
- Replace buzzing fluorescent tubes with other kinds of lighting.
- Use carpets or rugs on floors to reduce the noise of walking.
- Repair any noisy heating system components (e.g. worn out pumps).
- Keep doors to noisy rooms closed (rooms that may face a busy road or rooms such as the kitchen, which contain noisy equipment).
- Use lots of soft furnishings to absorb noise.

If noise is a problem for you, reduce the amount of red, orange and yellow in your home

- If possible, decorate the rooms of the noisy people in your home in pale, cool, quiet colours such as blue, green, grey and minimise the number of angles and points in the furniture, pictures or other decorative features (i.e. make them less agitating).

In general, if noise is a problem for you, reduce the amount of red, orange and yellow in your home, since these colours can cause agitation and increased sensitivity.

USING SOUND TO ENHANCE HARMONY

Noise does not necessarily have to be a negative aspect of your environment – it can actually be used to improve the sense of harmony in your home. We have already mentioned the idea of keeping tapes and CDs of relaxing sounds. Bird song can also be very calming, so place a bird-feeder or bird-bath close to the home to attract them. Some people like the sound of trickling water, although I find it unnatural and disturbing inside the home. There are a number of miniature water fountains that can be bought for use indoors, but check before you buy one that the sound of the electrical pump does not overwhelm the sound of the water.

Wind chimes can be an effective way of overriding other less pleasant sounds. There are a number of factors to consider however:

- Pitch: is a high pitched 'tinkle' from thin, short chimes, or a low pitched 'gong' sound from larger diameter chimes more comfortable for you?
- Volume: do not have a wind chime that is so loud that it annoys both you and the neighbours (keeping both of you awake on windy nights).
- Tone: wind chimes can be metal, ceramic or wood. The harsher, more penetrating tones are from metal chimes, while

wood (especially hollow bamboo) chimes have a softer tone.

- Size: if you hang a wind chime in a standard doorway or window opening, it would not be sensible to have a very large wind chime. It would either block out too much light or create an obstruction. Something small and discrete is usually adequate for urban homes.

Wind chimes have other purposes in feng shui. Shiny metal chimes are used symbolically to represent the warding off of unpleasant things and bad luck. For this they must be placed in quite specific locations in the home, but these depend on the direction the home faces and the current year. Full exploration of this subject is beyond the scope of this book but in my view it is secondary in importance to creating basic harmony in the home through the careful considerations of design that we have already described. A more practical use of wind chimes in feng shui is associated with the material element they represent. So if part of your home needs a more 'wood-type' energy, you might select a wooden wind chime for this space. (See chapter two for a comprehensive description of how different materials can influence the atmosphere in a room according to feng shui principles).

One more symbolic use of wind chimes is as a protection or warning signal of intrusion into your space, rather like the old-fashioned shop doorbell. Creating a sense of safety and security in your home is the subject of the next chapter.

Shiny metal chimes are used symbolically to represent the warding off of unpleasant things and bad luck

CHAPTER TWELVE

Safe and secure

To feel comfortable and at harmony in any home, we must feel safe and secure. There are some obviously dangerous conditions such as slippery floors, damaged electrical wiring, loose or broken floorboards, insufficient lighting and so on. I will assume that you do not need to be reminded of these, so let us look instead at some of the more subtle details of a typical home environment that can create a sense of unease or vulnerability in our subconscious minds.

Like so many of these subtle effects, one or two alone would probably not have measurable impact on your life, but it is the accumulation of subliminal stresses from many such subtle features over many months or years, that can have distinct consequences. So, if you feel insecure in any aspect of life (work, relationship, etc.) examine the ideas below for ways to enhance the 'atmosphere' of safety and security in your physical space, and very soon your feelings will begin to change. And when this happens, the external circumstances of your life have a tendency to change also.

OUTSIDE THE HOME

The most important aspect of security outside the home is the boundary of our space. This must be clearly defined, solid and intact. Broken fences, walls and hedges create a sense of exposure or vulnerability, even if you live in an area where the most fearful threat is from the neighbour's cat. Gates across a path or driveway at the boundary with the public road, also add to a sense of protection.

Ideally, the path or drive from the street to the main entrance to your home should not be a direct straight line. The symbolism here is that any enemies that may wish to venture towards your territory (tax inspectors, double-glazing salesmen, pizza-advert distributors, and so on) have no obstacles. Think of the moats around medieval cities. They were built in a zig-zag pattern so that it was harder for enemies to attack the city directly. If the path to your door is straight, and it is not possible to change it, place some plants close to, and slightly overhanging the path to give the illusion of breaking up the straight line.

What if there is not a path or driveway, and the main entrance to your house or flat opens directly on to a public thoroughfare? Here are some possibilities if you need to create a greater sense of security:

- Have good quality locks and bolts on the doors to the outside, and make a nightly routine of ensuring that all are used. There is the obvious intruder deterrent effect in this but, in addition, the act of locking and bolting the doors creates a mental feeling of security which has more general benefits – you are establishing in yourself the 'energy' of being safe and secure.
- Place statues of guardians either side of the front door. 'Guardians' could be fierce dogs, lions, warriors, etc. Of course if you live in an area where such items are likely to be stolen, you need to guard the guardians somehow; fix them

to the wall perhaps.

- A tall plant either side of the main door can have a similar effect to the guardians mentioned above. If the plants are not of the same height, place the taller one on the right side of the door as you face your home.
- Fix images or models of symbolic protectors to the front door such as a guardian angel or a lion-head door knocker.
- Hang a small wind chime just inside the door so that it makes a sound when the door is opened. This satisfies your mind that you will get an 'early warning' of someone entering the home and thus have time to prepare a defence if necessary. In feng shui we might instead have a wind chime with shiny reflective tubes outside the door to symbolically reflect back or disperse any negative influences on the home. A burglar alarm is probably much more effective in practice, but we sometimes have to pander to the needs of our primitive brain in order to actually feel really secure.
- Vulnerability is a more yin quality, while strength may be seen as more yang. Therefore increase the yang features of the main door by using light, strong colours, or railings with pointed tips near the entrance (pointed tips are 'fire'-shaped which is yang - see chapter two).

INSIDE THE HOME

Even within the boundaries of our own home, we may still feel insecure and unsettled. In order to harmonise our home, we need to remove any negative influences and introduce more positive ones.

People who live in high-rise flats may experience particular feelings of insecurity. One client lived on the fourteenth floor of a block of flats and was frequently troubled by dreams of falling. Her bedroom had several features that could have stimulated this condition. Firstly, the head of her bed was under a window, which could obviously be seen by the subconscious mind as a

Blue is the colour of water, the sky – everything that is not solid and stable

vulnerable position. Secondly, opposite the end of her bed was a large glass sliding door which led onto a small balcony and which gave quite a good bird's-eye view of the city. The floor in the bedroom had a blue carpet. Blue is the colour of water, the sky – everything that is not solid and stable. She also had a plant pot on a high shelf opposite the bed, with ivy hanging down from it. The range of solutions suggested included: turning the bed around so that the head was against a solid wall and where she would not face the balcony; closing the balcony door curtains at night; changing the carpet to a more earthy colour; removing the acrobatic plant pot; put large solid stone or earthenware flower pots in the room to increase the sense of stability.

This example gives many useful clues for improving the quality of sleep through creating, even symbolically, a more secure environment. You may also choose to do some of the following:

- Fix a solid headboard firmly to the bed.
- Avoid having anything (pictures, mirrors, shelves, etc.) on the wall above the head of the bed.
- Arrange the bed so that your head is as far as possible from the bedroom door.
- Don't sleep in a position where you can see your reflection in a mirror.
- If the head or foot of the bed is close to the bedroom door, place a small table or cabinet between the door and the bed to represent a protective barrier.

Many of these ideas also apply to any other space where you may like to rest and relax. For example in your living room, ensure that the chairs you relax in have high backs, that you do not sit with your back to the door or large window, that there are no heavy things hanging on the wall above your head, and so on.

Some other features that can contribute to feelings of insecurity or danger that I have seen in homes recently include:

- Stairs without banisters, or with very thin, weak-looking banisters.
- Stairs without risers between the treads.
- Very wide, floor-to-ceiling glass doors and windows. This can be very destabilising if at the front of the house. If you are in this situation, put some large or heavy objects (plant pots, statues, tables, etc.) in front of the glass.
- Glass shelves and glass-topped tables. We know that glass is a very brittle and fragile material, and the sight of weight on it troubles our subconscious mind. Also, glass shelves have quite sharp edges and are usually at a height where those edges 'attack' the eyes, throat, heart, stomach or even more sensitive parts!
- Kitchen knives hung in such a way that the blades are exposed and face the entrance to the kitchen.
- Sharp corners of cupboards, chimney breasts and so on, pointing at places where you either enter a room, or where you attempt to sleep or relax. In this situation, suppress the effect of the corner by putting a tall plant or lamp in front of it. Alternatively hang something such as a decorative wind chime or mobile on or near the corner so that your attention is distracted from it.

We have looked at a wide range of elements inside the home that can affect our sense of safety and security, but we can also be affected by what we see when we look out from our home to those areas controlled by other individuals, companies or local authorities. Such outside influences are discussed in the next chapter.

CHAPTER THIRTEEN

Outside influences

'No man is an island!' – so stated the poet John Donne (1572–1631). Similarly, no home is an island; it exists in an environment of other buildings and natural geological features. These influence to some degree the interaction between the home and the people who live in it simply because they can be seen, felt, smelt or heard from within the home environment. It is useful therefore to be aware of what these influences are so that we can encourage the beneficial ones and fend off the malevolent ones.

The main external aspects we will consider are:

- Topography: the shapes and size of the land and buildings around the home.
- Chi of the land: the degree of elegance and natural beauty around the home.
- Energy flow: the magnitude and direction of movement around the home, whether it is water, traffic, trains, aircraft or people.
- Landmarks: specific detailed elements of the landscape that can have significant subliminal effects.

TOPOGRAPHY

The shapes and size of the land and buildings around your home will affect the harmony within it. Traditional feng shui principles suggest that the most harmonious site for a home has rising ground at the back and on each side to 'protect' it, and a fairly open aspect to the front to allow you to see clearly what is coming towards you. This type of geographic configuration mirrors the secure cave-like situation our ancestors probably lived in. Animals and young children also tend to seek out hiding or resting places which have similar characteristics. The modern urban house or flat is unlikely to be surrounded by hills and valleys, all in the correct 'feng shui' places, so we need to make symbolic corrections to what is actually there.

If there is no support at the back of the home (e.g. it is on a site where the land slopes down from the rear of the property instead of up, or the home backs on to a large expanse of water, flat fields or a desert), a tall fence or trees at the back of the property will have a supportive effect provided that they are not too close – in which case they would become overbearing. Another tall building to the rear of the house can also serve the function of 'protector' unless it is a prison, nuclear power station, weapons factory, toxic chemical production plant, etc. In this case you may still need to plant trees to conceal the negative symbolism of these types of building.

In the case of a high-rise flat with large windows at the back, put some plants on the window-sills, or some solid, or solid-looking item such as a large stone, statue of an elephant – anything that represents solid protection. If you do not have windows at the back yet still feel the need for protection, hang a picture of hills or mountains on the back wall.

You can apply the same sort of ideas to protecting the sides of your home. A large hill, tall trees or buildings at the front of the home can create a feeling of being obstructed or blocked in life. You may also find it difficult to see clearly what to do or how to do it. If faced with this type of situation, one classic feng shui cure is to put a concave mirror (one that curves inwards) on the outside wall of the home, facing the offending edifice. A concave mirror inverts images, so by using such a device you are saying to your mind that the effect of the hill, tree or building is overturned, and will not affect you any more. This may sound like deluding oneself or brain-washing, but remember that the feeling of obstruction is also an illusion created by the mind, and if you delve into Buddhist or Taoist philosophy you will see that the entire universe is just as unreal.

CHI OF THE LAND

The appearance and quality of the land that surrounds your home is also important. If there are elegant gardens, spectacular views or other harmonious sights when you look out of your windows, consider placing a mirror in the room so that it reflects that image into the home. On the other hand, if you look out over a rubbish tip, car park, or other unnatural, uninspiring place, be sure not to position a mirror that would reflect this image into your room. If the view from your window is unattractive, it is especially important to create your own landscape, if possible by making your garden as beautiful as possible. You can also attract live energy such as birds by providing a feeder, bird-bath or nesting facilities. If you do not have a garden, make use of window-boxes or, failing that option, have lots of plants and flowers inside your home.

Create your own landscape

Attract live energy such as birds by providing a feeder, bird-bath or nesting facilities

ENERGY FLOW

The magnitude and direction of movement around the home, whether it is in the form of water, road traffic, trains, aircraft or people will influence the home environment. Traditional feng shui texts refer mostly to the flow of water, and give elaborate explanations about the good and bad aspects of house positions in relation to all kinds of watery channel configurations. However most of us do not live within sight of a fish pond, let alone a confluence of five rivers, but we can take the main underlying principle and apply it to the kinds of movements and flows that affect the typical urban or suburban home.

The fundamental idea is that when you look out of your doors or windows, any steady flowing phenomenon should ideally be moving towards your home, but not directly at it. This creates in the mind the idea that life is offering a continuous supply of good things, but is not actually attacking you with them. Conversely, if you usually see movement going away from you when looking out of your doors or windows, this suggests to the mind that life is depriving you of benefits and your vitality is draining away.

The most disturbing type of flow is that which comes directly at the main entrances or main windows of your home. This is most common in towns, where homes face a 'T' road junction. The effect is not so significant for quiet roads, but if the junction is busy, every time you look out of the window or the door something is coming at you or running away from you. A classic feng shui solution is to fix a convex mirror (one that curves outwards) to the front of your building, pointing at the disturbing traffic flow. By taking this action you are saying to your subconscious mind (which is the part that worries about the sight of things going from or coming at you) that any negative associations it may have concerning the traffic are being reflected back and dispersed. Alternatively, a shiny metal wind chime or other round, reflecting object with a convex surface (metal bowl, metal coated glass ball, etc.) placed inside the window, can serve the same purpose. It is the intention behind your action that counts, not so much the nature of the tool that you use.

The same technique can be applied if you live, as I do, close to a major airport and under the flight path of planes taking off or landing. Fix a convex mirror on the roof!

If you live on the inside bend of a road, railway or river, you are in a good position to see things coming your way in a non-aggressive manner. If you live on the outside of the bend however, take precautions to block views of traffic coming at, or going away from you. It is interesting to note that the outside bend of a river is more dangerous to live on because it is more likely to flood than the inside of the bend. Similarly, road accidents are more likely on the outside than the inside of a bend.

LAND MARKS

Specific detailed elements of the landscape can have significant subliminal effects and can upset your sense of harmony at home. These include:

- Lamp posts, telegraph poles, tree trunks, etc., directly opposite the main door and close to the house can be seen as threats by your subconscious mind. If possible, place some attractive object (plant, fountain, statue, etc.) between the house and the pole, to reduce its attention-grabbing effect.
- Some people associate churches and graveyards with sadness or even fear. If this applies to you, and you cannot block such a view from your home, it is possible to transform the effect into a more positive one. This is done by simply keeping healthy plants or fresh flowers in the windows from which you see the church or graveyard, or by putting images of young children or animals close by. In this way your mind begins to link growth and rebirth with the artefacts associated with spirituality and death.

- To symbolically reduce the effect of noisy pubs or clubs outside the home, use the convex-mirror trick. Also avoid having yellow or red paintwork on the door facing the pub or club, since these are energising colours and could encourage more noise. Blue has a calming effect. (See also chapter eleven on noise.)
- Other buildings may have features that produce subtle feelings of discomfort or unease. For example, if a sharp corner of a large house or building points directly at your main door or window, the subliminal mind can interpret such an image as potentially threatening. A similar effect can come from other features such as pointed or sharp-edged porticoes or roof designs, situated close to your home. Even worse are situations where raised sections of road or railway are built very close to, and cut right across, the windows of houses or flats. I think that architects and planners who create homes with such views should be sentenced to live in them for at least twenty years! Failing this kind of revenge, your best bet is again to use the small convex mirror discretely placed on or around the main door or window or, if possible, to create some visual barrier between your home and the offending structure.

You can benefit by becoming more aware of what is just outside your home

In general, what I am suggesting in this chapter is that you can benefit by becoming more aware of what is just outside your home, and what you actually feel (however faint and subtle the feeling) when you see, hear or smell it. Just this process of giving detailed attention to your environment, even if you judge it to be uninspiring, will help to defuse any subconscious irritations it may generate. If you can then take some physical action to counteract that effect, whether directly or merely symbolically, you are then harmonising the home with areas even beyond its own territory.

By now you may feel somewhat overwhelmed by all the possibilities for harmonising your home with your own needs and desires and with the surrounding area. It would be useful therefore to create a strategy for organising and prioritising what to do, and this is the subject of the last chapter – Taking steps.

CHAPTER FOURTEEN

Taking steps

Hands up all those who have read to this point in the book and still not found anything new to do to improve the harmony of their home. By the new, super advanced optical response and micro psycho-molecular feedback and transmission system, known only to Orion Books and secretly embedded behind the full stop at the end of the last sentence, I can see that no one has their hand up! This must mean that you all need to establish a plan for making these beneficial changes to your home. There are so many suggestions here that it may be difficult to know how to begin, so this chapter is intended to provide some guidelines for structuring your plan in the most efficient way.

Take a little time to get clear about the state of your own thoughts, feelings and emotions when at home

In fact, the arrangement of the chapters in this book is quite a good framework on which to begin, but you have already made the first and most important step, and that is to pick up this book in response to something on the cover that triggered a deeper desire, of which you may have been only vaguely aware.

The second step is to take a little time to get clear about the state of your own thoughts, feelings and emotions when at home. It may help to write these down. Feel free to express whatever comes to your mind; you don't have to show it to anybody. If you are at home right now, what are your primary feelings about your home or any other aspect of your life? If necessary you can use the feng shui ba-gua model described in chapter two (see page 14), as a guide to the nine key aspects of life. Bear in mind that if you are not used to looking closely at your thoughts, feelings and emotions, it may take a little practice and some courage to express them, even to yourself.

Step three is to imagine how you would really like to live. How would you participate in the world (through your job, charity work, etc.); what type and quality of relationships would you have; how would your home look, feel or smell? Again it may help to write down these ideas.

The fourth step is to have a really good look at your home; become conscious of what is there, what condition things are in, what you use or don't use. Take note of what your home looks like from the outside, and what you see when you look out of the window. Also be aware of how easy or difficult it is to move around the home, and how easy or difficult it is to find things. What smells and textures confront you when you enter the home? Are your chairs comfortable and do they give proper posture support? What are the most significant features of the pictures and other decorative objects around the house? Is the subject matter cheerful, pleasant and inspiring, or are they dull, meaningless or associated with negative feelings and emotions? Are the walls, floors or other flat surfaces covered with objects or are they barren, or somewhere in between? What is the dispersion and quality of natural and artificial light in each room of your home?

The idea here is to practise looking at your environment as if you were seeing it for the first time and to notice all the little details that you may have habitually ignored. It is these details that can give you the key to creating the harmonious home that you desire. During this process it is quite likely that the same type of phenomenon will recur in several parts of the home. For example, if the hallway is cluttered, it is probable that the lounge, bedroom and kitchen are also cluttered. 'Clutter' is therefore a common theme in your life and this is where you should start the harmonising process.

Step five is to make more space for yourself as described in chapter three. Removing unnecessary physical obstructions in your home is the key to removing emotional or mental blockages in your life. Without going through this process it is much harder to see what other steps are necessary to harmonise your home and the other components of your life. You may not be able to clear out everything at once, so you will probably have to revisit this step from time to time while following other phases of the harmonisation process. In fact, we should all purge and 'make space' frequently, to avoid the accumulation of possessions and the constriction of energy conduits in our homes, and subsequently in our lives.

'Make space' frequently, to avoid the accumulation of possessions and the constriction of energy conduits

You may also at this time, make a point of removing any images and symbols that do not contribute to harmony (see chapter seven), and dealing with any obvious aspects that can impart a sense of anxiety or insecurity, as described in chapter twelve.

With a clearer view of our homes, it is now appropriate to take step six. This is to create the best first impressions and last impressions that we can, using the ideas described in chapter four. There are two potential places to start on this aspect of harmonisation – either the front of the home (front wall, garden, front door and exterior) or the bedroom. If you are not sleeping well, or you are waking up feeling more tired than when you went to bed, or you experience persistent bouts of illness, I would recommend that you get to work on your bedroom as soon as possible. This is also a good place to start if it is not possible to make significant improvements to the front of the home (perhaps because you live in a block of flats, or because there is nothing you can do without the assistance of a mechanical digger, a couple of cement mixers and a small army of builders). If none of these circumstances apply, and you have a house where the front garden is a mess and the paint is peeling off the front door, I would tend to begin there and migrate to the bedroom when the front of the house is in reasonably good order.

When working on your bedroom it is important to take note of the critical points made on geopathic stress (chapter eight), colour (chapter six), images and symbols (chapter seven), and the use of non-toxic materials (chapter nine). These are especially important if you have trouble sleeping or if you are ill.

With the front of the home and your bedroom sorted out, it is now time to harmonise the entrance hall and bathroom, but bear in mind the following caveat. If you normally enter or leave the home other than through the main door or hallway, (such as via the kitchen and back door) you need to harmonise this area as well.

The next phase of harmonisation, step seven, is to establish a strategy for dealing with all remaining areas of your home – including the garden if you have one. I would tend to start with the kitchen, since this is generally the source of nourishment for your physical body. Food prepared in a harmonious atmosphere somehow tastes better and feels more energising than food prepared in a stressful space. The best way to approach this part of your harmonisation program is to consider each room separately, but with an eye on what the effect might be on the overall home. First of all, be clear about how you want to use the room. Then briefly review the other chapters in the book for clues as to how best to make design and decor really work for you. Categorise the options you come up with into:

A Things to be done that cost nothing or very little in terms of time or money.

B Actions that will cost a significant, but not overwhelming amount.

C Changes that require a major investment.

> *The physical feelings associated with thoughts of excitement are the same as those for fear*

Do the category A tasks first, see the effect, then consider other actions. It may be a good idea to do all the category As in each room before going further with category B or C items.

If you have conscientiously worked through steps one to six, plus the the category A tasks of step seven, your home will be now be in very good shape. You can continue with category B or C work if time and finances allow, but you may also like to start embarking on ways to energise or stimulate some of the specific results you want to see in your life. This is step eight. To begin you need to go way back to step two, where you wrote down the new experiences or changes that you desire. If you are wondering what to focus on initially, look for what interests and excites you the most. Trust that the Universe or God does not create pointless and extraneous things, so if you feel a strong excitement or intention about something, that is a good indication as to the direction in which you should be heading. Be aware however that the physical feelings associated with thoughts of excitement are the same as those for fear. So, if your desires do not hurt you or anyone else (either physically or emotionally), then you are acting from pure excitement. Otherwise, fear is the driving force and this will not have good results.

Let us assume that you have selected an area or aspect of life with which you would like to be in more harmony. Identify which segment of the ba-gua model described in chapter two (see page 14), is associated with your objective. From this it is easy to see which areas of the home or of any individual room are assigned to represent this aspect of life. Now choose a method of energising that space or of clearly marking your intentions.

To energise a space you could add extra lighting, burn candles, add a picture or other object with lots of bright red or gold in it, add a bright mobile, or something which has some movement such as fish in a tank or a clock with a second hand or pendulum. If there is a window there you could hang a multi-faceted glass ball to catch and refract sunlight, or put a healthy plant or bright flowers there.

To mark your intentions, choose some symbol or image that represents what you want. There are several examples of this in chapter seven. Be imaginative and creative. The more you think about what really represents what you want, the stronger your intentions become. Your mind will soon get the message and start working away in the background to drive you in the right direction.

WARNING – It is best to do steps one to seven before moving on to step eight, otherwise you are in danger of energising what you don't want, or at least having a less-than-optimum result!

Now your sense of being in harmony with your home and life in general will start changing. As one issue is resolved, others will emerge. Step nine is therefore about remaining conscious of what is happening, and running through the steps again and again to make yet more adjustments as time goes on. You may then like to look deeper into the principles and methods of feng shui and to become familiar with more refined approaches to harmonising your home and your life. (@)

I wish you the best of success, and harmony in every aspect of your life.

Where can I find...?

Throughout this book there are many references to further information that could not be included in this text. Such references are marked with the symbol – (@).

I am compiling a separate catalogue of this additional data which contains:

- manufacturers or suppliers of particular products or services.
- detailed descriptive data on products and how to use them.
- evaluations of product performance.
- further recommended reading on particular subjects.

The subjects covered include:

- feng shui – books, workshops, consultations, organisations.
- dowsing – books, courses, consultations, organisations.
- electromagnetic field neutralising equipment and geopathic stress.
- colour use and planning.
- lighting systems.
- harmonisation and clearing strategies.
- feng shui principles, models, tools and techniques.
- sources of natural household and personal care products.
- sources of feng shui recommended tools (energising items, images and symbols, etc.)
- feng shui for business and corporate identity.
- designing your self-build home.

If you would like a copy of this catalogue please write to: Integral Dynamics UK, PO Box 24422, London W5 4GY, UK, or call (0) 20 8840 9688 or e-mail gg@intedyn.co.uk

APPENDIX

Feng shui astrology year-type numbers

9	8	7	6	5	4	3	2	1
1928	1929	1930	1931	1932	1933	1934	1935	1936
1937	1938	1939	1940	1941	1942	1943	1944	1945
1946	1947	1948	1949	1950	1951	1952	1953	1954
1955	1956	1957	1958	1959	1960	1961	1962	1963
1964	1965	1966	1967	1968	1969	1970	1971	1972
1973	1974	1975	1976	1977	1978	1979	1980	1981

also available from

THE ORION PUBLISHING GROUP

- ☐ **Apples & Pears** £3.99
  GLORIA THOMAS
  0 75281 604 7
- ☐ **Are You Getting Enough?** £4.99
  ANGELA DOWDEN
  0 75281 702 7
- ☐ **Arousing Aromas** £3.99
  KAY COOPER
  0 75281 546 6
- ☐ **Body Foods For Women** £6.99
  JANE CLARKE
  0 75280 922 9
- ☐ **Coping With Your Premature Baby** £4.99
  PENNY STANWAY
  0 75281 596 2
- ☐ **Cranks Recipe Book** £6.99
  CRANKS RESTAURANTS
  1 85797 140 X
- ☐ **Eat Safely** £3.99
  JANET WRIGHT
  0 75281 544 X
- ☐ **Entertaining with Cranks** £6.99
  CRANKS RESTAURANTS
  0 75282 579 8
- ☐ **Food** £6.99
  SUSAN POWTER
  0 75280 315 8
- ☐ **The Good Mood Guide** £4.99
  ROS & JEREMY HOLMES
  0 75282 584 4
- ☐ **Health Spa at Home** £3.99
  JOSEPHINE FAIRLEY
  0 75281 545 8
- ☐ **Juice Up Your Energy Levels** £3.99
  LESLEY WATERS
  0 75281 602 0
- ☐ **Kitchen Pharmacy** £7.99
  ROSE ELLIOT & CARLO DE PAOLI
  0 75281 725 6
- ☐ **A Natural History of the Senses** £7.99
  DIANE ACKERMAN
  1 85799 403 5
- ☐ **The Natural Way To Stop Snoring** £4.99
  DR ELIZABETH SCOTT
  0 75280 067 1
- ☐ **The New Cranks Recipe Book** £6.99
  NADINE ABENSUR
  0 75281 677 2
- ☐ **Sensitive Skin** £4.99
  JOSEPHINE FAIRLEY
  0 75281 547 4
- ☐ **Spring Clean Your System** £3.99
  JANE GARTON
  0 75281 601 2
- ☐ **Stop the Insanity!** £6.99
  SUSAN POWTER
  1 85797 323 2
- ☐ **Vegetarian Slimming** £6.99
  ROSE ELLIOT
  0 75280 173 2

All Orion/Phoenix titles are available at your local bookshop or from the following address:

Littlehampton Book Services
Cash Sales Department L
14 Eldon Way, Lineside Industrial Estate
Littlehampton
West Sussex BN17 7HE
telephone 01903 721596, *facsimile* 01903 730914

Payment can either be made by credit card (Visa and Mastercard accepted) or by sending a cheque or postal order made payable to *Littlehampton Book Services*.

DO NOT SEND CASH OR CURRENCY.

Please add the following to cover postage and packing

UK and BFPO:
£1.50 for the first book, and 50p for each additional book to a maximum of £3.50

Overseas and Eire:
£2.50 for the first book plus £1.00 for the second book and 50p for each additional book ordered

---

BLOCK CAPITALS PLEASE

name of cardholder ....

....

address of cardholder ....

....

....

....

postcode ....

delivery address (if different from cardholder)

....

....

....

....

postcode ....

☐ I enclose my remittance for £..............................

☐ please debit my Mastercard/Visa (delete as appropriate)

card number ☐☐☐☐☐☐☐☐☐☐☐☐☐☐☐☐

expiry date ☐☐☐☐

signature ....

prices and availability are subject to change without notice